# How Many Miracles Can I Have?

**By**

**Dr. Earline Cotton aka Mama Soul**

ISBN: 0-7596-7468-X

This book is printed on acid free paper.

1stBooks - rev. 1/24/02

I can remember my mom telling me that the streets where lined with ambulance as her voice trembled and her eyes filled with tears. She said she knocked on the door so hard and screamed so loud that it should have woke the dead. Mom said she was crying and yelling at the same time. She had been to a club meeting. Mom belong to a club with some of her friends. They wore green skirts and white blouses very pretty dark green tailored skirts. Mom had very fair skin with freckles; she was German Irish about five, six large frame very well proportion. In all the right places if you know what I mean. I have never seen mom wear slacks of any kind she said ladies didn't and don't wear pants. When she came home from one of her meetings. My brothers, and sisters and I was at home.all of us were unconscious, in a big living room chair that was in one of the bedrooms.Some slept holding each other on bunk beds. Mom said she was so scared she had lost her babies. She said she called out our names of 12 children 6 boys 6 girls as they picked us up and carried us out to the awaiting ambulances. She said she couldn't stop shaking and praying. We lived in East Saint Louis Mo. In what is known as a shot gun house, for those that doesn't know, if you stand in the front door you can see all the way throughout the house.

All the way in the back yard, on the back porch was the outhouse, We didn't have a bathroom like most of you know, in the house with lights and toilet that flushes.

We had a back porch with an outhouse shed on it. A shed is three walls and a door. Ours was made of old scrap wood not a solid foundation. Just a shed with as few nails as possible, No smooth nice finish wood on any part of this place. In the shed was a long board with a whole in it, no lights couldn't flush it. When you sat down if you were not careful, you could get a splendor. In a very bad spot if you know what I mean. In the dirt back yard was a big metal tub which was for bathing in the summer and washing clothes and for making lye soap. Mom was a very smart lady that had a lot of responsibility, which she carried her part plus.she took care of us as best as she knew how. Mom would get up early sometimes it would still be dark and make a fire under the tub fill the tub with water Washing our clothes in the lye soap water mom made boiling hot. No washing machine unless you call a scrub board or washing board a machine.

Call us including mom the motor we washed by hand and a scrub board. Mom did most of the washing as I remember. The older brothers and sisters hung out the clothes, help to bath the younger ones. I love the smell of fresh clean clothes hanging out side to dry. Then Mom had times she would iron our clothes. First she had sprinkles them with water, and folded them they would be damp. We had lots of clothes we shared and didn't mind sharing. Not out loud, we did want mom or dad to hear. Or you couldn't set down for a while with out a pillow.

Getting back to what happen, we used coal for everything including cooking and heat. We had two stoves that used the coal one was in the kitchen and was made of iron with four round holes with lids to cook on top of. And a heavy iron oven door with a big oven that was not big enough mom always said when she cooked. To heat the stove you had to put coal under the lids on top of the stove and under the oven to heat the oven. Daddy would take small pieces of wood and ball up paper and make a layer of it and add the coal. Daddy really knew how to make a fire; it would be red hot. Mom made hers a little different she used more wood chips than Dad did, but hers was just as hot. They always said keep the little ones away from the stove. And that it was very dangerous. But this night, first we got hungry and tried to start a fire in the coal stove in the kitchen the stove was a tall stove hard to reach but of course we found a way.

We went out side and gathered small pieces of wood we found. We finally got, the wood and coal to start the fire and if you didn't put the led on all the way coal gas smoke, which is very toxic. Would get it out and of course it was poison, yes mom said don't touch the stove, and was not freezing out side but It was cold. first we got under the cover to keep warm but that was not enough for us, cant you just see these kids from about sixteen to two the last two children had not been born. Let me also explain that this house had four rooms to the right was a small room we called a bedroom to the right was a room we called mom's bedroom and living room the middle room was the big bedroom where most of us slept; we had a potbelly stove in there also, a cast iron stove, that helped to heat the whole house. The people rushed in to get us out of the house to the waiting ambulance we had to go to Saint-Louis to the hospital we didn't have a hospital for BLACKS in East Saint Louis. The doctor said a minute longer and we would all been dead, HOW MANY MIRACLES CAN I HAVE? I can remember now at night when Mom would set the fire to last all night; the potbelly stove in the big bedroom would be red hot our bunk beds were up against the wall about ten feet away from the stove on the left side It could have been a little further, of the room was a closet a very small one. When she would send us to bed and turn out the lights. I wanted to be the first one sleep because when everyone was sleep I would open My eyes, And a lady in a long black dress very soft and smooth looking that fit her like a glove. It seem to flow over her body, but very ladies like, if you know what I mean. She had jet black long weave hair. Her hair was gently pulled back in a bun not a hair out of place. Smooth chocolate brown skin In front of her was a large German shepherd dog. The dog had a thick spiked collar around his neck with Hugh Spikes a very large chain hooked onto the collar, the lady was holding the chain very gently the dog was setting very still not a sound did he udder. The first time I saw her I screamed my mom came rushing into the room asking what was the matter I ask her did she see the lady? when she turned the light on the lady was gone. She looked in the small closet in the room and said there is no one here, now go back to sleep. I pulled the cover over my head she turned out the light and went back to bed.

I tried to get my sisters and brothers to wake up with me.

But to no avail, sometimes the lady and dog would come back when Mom would go back to bed, night after,

Night this would go on. I believe I was about seven when the lady came I started seeing the lady before the accident.

With the poison gas from the coal stove in the kitchen. One day I was playing out side and it was about sun down outside you know gray like just before dark. I started thinking its going to be getting dark soon, and it will be time for bed. I know the lady will come, what does she want? Is she real? I know she is, because I'm not sleep when she comes, just every one but me is. This time I will touch the lady and see what happens. This was after the lady and dog had come every night for a few weeks.

Sure enough soon mom said come in and wash up for bed she had heated some water on the stove for us. She poured the hot water in a wash basin and we washed up changing the water as it got dirty by throwing it out the back door out by the garden away from the back door.

Then we would line up to go out on the back porch sometimes with a flash lights yes we did have them to use the outhouse before going to bed. Sometimes mom would tuck us in sometimes tell us a bedtime story then out went the lights and when all was a sleep, then the lady with the dog came. Always the same dress the dog was always on the chain this time I spoke to her. And she answered me back in a voice like no other I have heard very soft and gentle. You could hear the love In her voice, as she said don't be afraid I will not hurt you. Then I fell off to sleep feeling very good inside and safe. I can't explain why I felt this way until years later. The next night,

When the lady came I got out of bed and walked slowly over to her as she said so gently please don't come any closer.I knew the potbelly iron stove was red hot.I could feel the heat on my body as I tried to get closer.

I tried to reach for the lady she said no don't and the dog started to bark I ran back to bed as Mom said Earline what are you doing? who are you talking to? I said I'm talking to the lady Mom said, what lady? and if I didn't go to sleep she was coming in the room that was a promise she would keep and I am the one that would be sorry.

If you know what I mean, I stopped talking the lady and dog would just stand there when I woke up the next morning she was gone. after the accident I don't know how many times she came after that, this house sometimes was such a house of plenty joy we would all set around the kitchens table and eat whatever mom was cooking. If it was Friday it was fried fish and spaghetti and potato salad my mother was a great cook! And like a lot of families some times it was just ho cakes and gravy or syrup and biscuits hot out the oven, made from scratch, but you would be full and happy thank God, A ho cake is a big biscuit in case you didn't know. Sometimes Daddy would go to the slaughter house and get meat cheap Pig ears, pig feet, chitterlings these are food we didn't have to pay for, meat that most white people didn't want or know was good. Yes we had roast, pork chops some beef too. Chicken was all most always Sunday dinner fixed a variety of ways, all of which I loved and still do. When we had plenty we would eat and finished everything on our plates, and try to get up from the table, daddy would say where are you going? we would say daddy we are full he would say come around here and he would fill our stomachs and say you're not full goes eat some more.

Sometimes we would be so good and full we would fall asleep at the table I think that made Daddy felt good when he could feed us well. Times were hard for a man who was never taught formal EDU. I mean it was hard for Black man to find work Daddy never gave up, Daddy was a policy man he wrote numbers, I don't know what you call it now. But he made It okay he tried very hard to take care of us. We didn't have welfare to help us when Daddy was working and fell off the back of a cement truck and hurt his back. You didn't have to have the protection for workers like you have now especially Black workers. So daddy became a policy man. I remember daddy wearing a back brace and sometimes he would moan when he tried to get up from setting down. Daddy was not a man that lay around the house he was always trying to make ends meet. Sometimes he couldn't stand straight his back hurt so badly. He never complained I just remember him moaning and mom saying Forthune why don't you stay home? He said we have to have money to feed these children he would say. We lived on a dead end street at the end of the street was a paint factory. At noon when the whistle would blow the men that worked there would come out with all different color paint, it smelled bad but the colors were bright and Pretty. Red, blue, orange, pink, yellow of course all the workers were White. We would sit on the porch and watch them come out.

Even their faces had paint on them. The factory was only about three houses from us, at the dead end of the street, we didn't think of the fact that we didn't see any Blacks come out.

We just looked at the colors, before the factory was railroad tracks we would run to the tracks and look at the men sometimes they would laugh and would say things to each other we didn't and couldn't under stand them, we had to be careful and not get on the tracks because the trains would come so fast and daddy and mom said stay away from the tracks. I remember one of my brothers went into a boxcar on the train one night. It was just setting there, and it was full of bananas. I think we were sick from eating so many of them. Of course our parents didn't find out, but they could tell we had been up to something. Or had eaten something that didn't agree with us, because we stayed in the outhouse most of the time for a day or two.

On the left side of the street Black people, lived on the right side whites lived the white lady.

That lived in the corner house looked at us liked we were dirt she would frown at us some times we would speak she never said anything except the N word. She was a large frame.

Women with shoulder length hair I can't remember if she was what you would call pretty; she was the same color as my mom that's why I didn't understand her hatred for us. She acted so mean I never thought about it too much. A couple of houses down on the same side of the street lived a man named Dennis with his mother when he would pass us outside playing he was a very nice looking Black man well dressed very neat, He would call my sister Lavonda mom big stockings because she had big pretty legs and Me he called me red red the cabbage head because of my red hair and moon eyes because I had big eyes. I said when I got big I was going to beat him up. I didn't know that he was just kidding us. His mom was a church going women.

She went to church every Sunday and before she went she cooked her Sunday dinner and put the pies and cake in the window to cool. It smelled so good you could smell the sweet potato pie.the chicken and dressing with all the spices, the greens, fresh made corn bread that almost taste like cake. The winds blowing these sweet smells down to our windows and door. My stomach started to rumble and turn. My mouth started to water and drawl. If you were not hungry you would be after you smelled this, because it taste as good as it smelled. I knew because she had given us some of her cooking before. One Sunday mom and daddy was gone, we made a ladder out of boxes and went in through the window and took the whole dinner.

After we ate it, then we got scared. I said don't tell are we will not be able to set for a month. We hid the pots and pans under our front steps. After we had eaten then we felt guilty, for what we had done, and was scared. When our parents came back we didn't tell them what we had done. We were so scared I guess the lady called the police we didn't take anything but the dinner, the police came to our house they scared us so bad they said they would take us down town and lock us up. We started crying and begging them not to take us please. I don't know what they said to our parents, Mom seemed a little frightens and I could tell her and Daddy had an argument. Everybody told on me, I was right in the middle of it with my brothers. So I had to take the police to the steps and show them where the pots and pans were. I was so scared I said I would never do anything like that again. The lady forgave us after our parents made us go to her house, and tell her we were sorry. And we would not do it again. And we couldn't sit down for a while. My mom took three switches and braided them together tight and gave us a good whopping with the switches. Lined us up and you better not run or it was worse. Thank God Mom had pity on us because we really didn't want to cause her problems. She said that's okay and the next day she let us go out and play. We would go down to the corner On the right hand side of the street, was an empty lot with some patch of short weeds.

Mostly dirt, my brothers and sisters loved to play baseball in the lot. Or stick balls or just play tag. On our side of the street across from the lot, at the corner was a house, a big pretty green lawn cut even and trimmed and a very nice and clean house out side with a fence around it. A wire fence, In this yard was a big bull dog. The dog would run to the fence and bark as you pass by. He looked real scary to us the dog would make me angry sometimes, I would get a stick and tease him thinking he could never reach me.

Just being a kid I would get closer and closer one time I got a little to close and the dog bit me on the leg. You would have thought my leg was coming off.I like to had a fit, I screamed and hollered my brother Tony and Lavonda my sister came running first across the street to see what happen to me. All the rest came running over across the street to see what happen to me, they were yelling what happen? What happen? I said the dog bit me.

They ran home ahead of me screaming and hollering mama.she came out of the house.

Saying my baby! My baby! Mom was so mad she went to the house with the dog. She was walking so fast that she was almost running. Her face was very red that meant she was boiling mad. The owner who was a white mans and was not friendly to us Blacks, said he didn't understand the dog didn't just bit people and how did he bit me? He said I must have been doing something. mama said were you doing anything? I said no mama. I was not bothering that old dog he just jumped up and bit me. I didn't tell mom what really happen. I knew I would be in trouble with her if I did. As you can tell I was always getting into trouble, The bit was not really that bad and it was on the back of my leg. If you haven't guessed by now I am the middle child. Here I go again a girl that lived on our street named litha, she had come from a large family also, but they had two working parents and dresses a little better than we did. Both her parents were Black, not like mine so we were not excepted by either side.We looked like a beautiful rainbow from dark blonde hair to jet-black hair. Weave hair to curly hair to straight hair. This girl and I would always fight. She was tall and skinny and to me she was very pretty. I have no idea why we argued and fight, she would always put her finger in my face. And I told her she would do that one-day and I would bit it off. I guess she didn't think fat meat was greasy, and one day she stuck her finger in my face and I tried to bit it off, Here I go again in trouble again her mom came to our house and told my mom she was going to have to pay the doctor bill. My mom gave me a good whipping for that I guess you could say we were kids and we got into all kinds of things. Mama would sit.

On what I called a porch, which was a long concrete slab, that went from our side of the house to the neighbor's house. It may sound long, but it was not, but long enough for a swing on it. When it was warm she would sit in the swing and comb and braid our hair. My sisters had some long and thick hair. Mine was not as long as their hair, we had Green eyes, brown eyes, gray eyes. From white complexion to chocolate we are a melting pot of a beautiful rainbow of color mom was a big-boned woman of about five feet five very fair complexion with freckles with a very pretty smile. She was very pretty period. I remember ounce my Brother was teasing me, and was pulling on my ribbon. Just like kids I went inside and told my mother.

She dressed him up with ribbon in his hair, and made him sit on the porch. He was so mad at me he didn't speak to me for a long time. And I didn't blame him I felt so bad and still do when I think about it. But believe me no matter what we looked out for each other, and were very close especially in time of trouble. I remember once mom was gone and it seems like that is when I would really get hungry I went into the kitchen and fixed a mustard and onion sandwich and I was teasing my brothers and sisters with it. Tony asks is it good Earline? I said its real good.

He said are you sure? I said hmmm it's so good. So he went into the kitchen and fixed Him one.A little while later he started moaning and saying his stomach was hurting. I said OH LORD! What have I done? mom come into the house calling my name EARLINE!

What have you done now? I said he just ate a mustard and onion sandwich like I did, mom rushed him to the hospital, his appendix had burst. They always teased me saying I made Tony sick. Our parents deceived we needed to be on a farm we were getting into so much mischief, and the neighbors were complaining that we were home alone a lot, I don't know what if any thing happen. Other than by this time, a couple of my older brothers and one sister left on there own. I have no idea how that came about.

But off we went to Adams Wis. It was seven miles to the country store and to school which we walked the seven miles most of the time. In the summer it was hot and dry walking down the dirt roads, we just kept going, or we would get a whipping when we got home. In the winter our feet would be almost frost bitten by the time we got to school. We walked home from school to. The winter was the worse because in the afternoon it was colder, because the sun had gone down. Sometimes we would be crying, by the time we got home. Mom would rub our feet fast and hard to get the circulation back into them. And some times put them into a bucket of Ice cold water we would just cry.

We went to a one room school house, about three or four grades was in one room.It might have been as many as fifteen kids.oh yea we were the only Blacks. But I never heard the N word at school or home I remember an Indian man coming to our house and giving us a German Shepherd dog he was beautiful and big I believe it was our first pet. We called him Shep. We really loved him he was our first pet. He went ever where with us. He made the walk to school fun. He would go winter or summer and wait out side for us to come out. Not too much was different about this house except you had to step down to go into the kitchen. It the stove was a coal burning stove no different than our other one.

The outhouse was further away from the house and dark and scary no lights in the out house.

We learned how to plant a garden, and milk a cow, dig up potatoes, kill the potato bugs, and gather the eggs from the chicken coop, we would watch, as mom would wring a chicken's neck. put it in a tub of water she was boiling after it died, and plucked the feathers off, clean the insides.

Get it ready for dinner along with veggies from our own garden at least here we had plenty of good fresh food to eat. We had this big wooden churn, for putting the milk in and moving this stick up and down after, what seem like your arm was going to fall off. this white creamy butter would come to the top. hmmmmm good. We didn't have this before fresh homemade butter.

My dad would talk to the neighbor up the road, and the Indian man that would stop by. I don't know where he lived and they would share with daddy, telling him how to plant and plow the field. Milk the cows and he would teach us kids how to work, it was hard work but what we got in return was well worth it.

He would work long and hard in the fields. And soon my brothers would go with him once or twice. But daddy didn't have much patience to teach, and would tell them to come and work the garden with us. Once I don't know why but, I got very sick with a high fever we had no money for the hospital but mom just kept putting cold towels and I remember her praying to GOD to help me I don't know how long I was sick about a week. I remember being hot and weak feeling sleepy.

I remember getting better and joining the FOUR H CLUB I took some flour sacks and by hand made a skirt and won first place ribbon.My family was so pleased. Then I listening as my mom was reading the paper to my dad whom she often did daddy couldn't read. I didn't know until years later. After we were all grown and had traveled many roads with dad.

Anyway mom was reading to dad and us about this girl about my age who had written to the President who was Eisenhower a light went off in my head why can't I do it and get a home for us bigger and in a town, and I did of course he responded, and when the letter came guess whose name was called as soon as the letter came? You are right mine. Soon after we moved to Madison Wis. Let me share with you something that happen back in East Saint Louis Mo. Before we moved to Adams I can remember daddy taking us for a ride we would be all dressed up hair combed ribbons in the hair boys all neat. In what seemed like the worlds longest station wagon with wood on the side this white man pulled up along side us as we were riding and singing songs and laughing, and called daddy the N Word and called us Little pickanenee. Daddy chase that man down, we thought we would have an accident. Daddy was a very good driver. He made the other car pull over. Daddy got out and went to the mans car, the man was a white man who seemed shocked that daddy pulled him over. Daddy carried a long switch blade knife daddy made the man stop. And said what did you call my children? I never seen so many colors.

On one face before in life. mom was in the car calling Forthune! Fortune! don't do anything please. Mom said don't hurt him, don't hurt him, daddy came back in the car and we went back to enjoying our ride. Mama laugh at daddy trying to help him get over his anger. Its sometimes hard to tell you things in order, life is not always in order. I can be thinking something and my mind will flash back or ahead I hope you can follow me I want you to understand what I'm trying to share with you I pray this will be a blessing to all who read Amen? Back to the move to Madison we had a very big house. It was first floor and second floor, the second floor had three or four bedrooms plus a large bathroom. The first floor had at least one large bedroom and a living room a kitchen dining room a bath room on both floors inside the house we had hot and cold running water a real wash sink in each real inside bathroom with electricity, with faucets of hot and cold water. Of course we were a little older my older Brothers and sisters started dating and going to parties. While in Madison I meet a young man fell madly in love and ran away to be with him, thank

GOD he was a very nice young man and never touch me. He was in the Army and scared out of his wits as I think back on it he I believe was about twenty. I think I was about twelve or thirteen, and I really loved him and I think I still love him a little today. He was a milk chocolate brown smooth complexion. Soft spoken tender brown eyes that lit up when he looked at me. Medium build very firm body walked with such strong steps. Smelled fresh all the time and would set and hold me with such tenderness. Finally convinced me to go back home and we talked to my parents and they said we could get married.

After he left I got in big trouble with them, I never seen him again. I often think, what would my life have been like, if I married him oh well we will never know. A couple of years later things, at home changed we moved to Milwaukee, WIC. Mom started sending us to church, she didn't like to go she said.I believe it was she felt she would be treated different because of her color. But I remember her going with me to church in Madison, and being baptized in the lake with me. I felt so close to her I cant remember how I got her to do it Miracle! Of my Heavenly Father. See there I go again, going back to something that happen before. My dad and mom started not getting along and they broke up. I stayed home about a year after that and then I left home.

I went to Chicago with someone I thought was a friend but he had other ideas. I really was not very smart about men and still not. We stayed at a rooming house, which was very popular back then.he wanted to have sex with me. I said no, he left me, and when the rent came due I had no money.so I had to leave, I had not found a job, so at night I slept in cars that people left open. And tried to wake and get out before they came out to there cars. When I would get caught they that would yell at me. And I would get out running, thank GOD for Miracles! I would wash up in gas stations and change clothes that I carried in a paper bag I had some at the greyhound bus station in a locker but I had to be careful not to get caught because I was a run a way. I finally got a job in a beauty salon cleaning and shampooing ladies when I could, because back then you could not work on a customer unless you had a license. While at the shop a young man that was a beautician taught me how to wear makeup how to wear my hair and how to do my nails. I had found another rooming house to live. I did nails in the shop. And did all right; I didn't have boyfriends at this time I was just trying to live. I worked as a waitress, barmaid, I lied about my age managed a candy section in a department store. When I caught my boss stealing I reported it to headquarters and came up with an idea for busted bags of candy and got the job of department head. I worked long and hard hours until I quit the job.

Sitting on steps of my house on day I saw Joe Louis I didn't know it was him until his driver got out and came over and said that Mr. Louis wanted to meet me.I was thrilled, he owned some apartments across the street and we went out once. When he found out I was under twenty-one I never seen him again. He was a very nice person and a gentleman. While working as a barmaid I had to stuff my bra I didn't have enough up they're to me. Mom came to see me while I was a barmaid she was not happy about it but she let me stay I called the owner Uncle Mix because only his relatives could work for him. I was making a good living and most of the men that came in the bar played the horses and I think they were afraid of Uncle Mix in some way so they were only polite to me but tipped me very. I really liked my play uncle he was nice but I learn fast and worked hard I was always a good worker if I must say so my self. I was setting at a restaurant one day having lunch. When a man tried to talk to me. And when I didn't respond he got up and slapped me. Very hard in my face I was shocked and scared the people in the restaurant acted like they were afraid of him. I called the police but I didn't know his name or anything so that was the end of that. Finally someone came into the club that was allowed to ask me out after getting Uncle Mix's permission first. He was a man in his late twenties I believe he was a gambler and still living at home with his mother which should have told me something. He would come over to my rooming house and we would talk we didn't go anywhere after a while he stayed the night and wanted to stay more I told him I didn't believe in living together and didn't want sex before marriage. I really had feelings for him as I look back on it but I don't think I was in love I was just lonely. I wanted to be treated special, which he did. I told my mother I couldn't live without him and she signed for us to marry. Little did I know this was a rebound for him he was really in love with the girl across the street and she came over after we married to his moms where we lived to see me and see what I was about. My husband was not home when she came. But his mom and sister and brother were. She asks to see me. My husband came in and asks her what was she doing there? She said I just wanted to see my rival they had words and she left, I called my mom she said come home, which I did. I went home to Mil. And stayed with mom and the family that was left at home, most had left for all kinds of reasons it was about six at home. I tried to talk to my husband on the phone. But it was over after about six months of marriage. Which made me sad, but I went on and got a divorce. My husband was a very sweet man spoke softly and a good man and I will not beat up on him today. We cant help who we love I cant say if he loved me or not or if I just said No!

Just because we didn't make it does not mean he wasn't a good man. This story is not about beating up on family and friends this is a story about how many Miracles can I have By the Grace of GOD. About the love of GOD for his children and how he will be there and is there even when you don't know it or him. I knew of him but didn't know him and what he could do and how he could help and do all things. We can do all things Through Christ who strengthin us (Phil: 4:13). After a while I went back to Chicago got a job met a man he also lived with his mom he was not working at the time I would go back and forth to Mil. And Chicago we seem to get very serious he was a lot of fun he would work when he could find a job he had a police record it was hard to find work. Finally I seen this relationship was not for me and tried to leave he got angry and said he would kill me if left I knew he could be violent if he wanted to but I got away with the help of my friends and went back to Mil. For a while after being there for about six months I meet someone and we dated and started living together yes living together. I got pregnant and he ask me to marry him even though his family was not happy about it I came from the wrong side of the tracks we didn't own our home we rented my mom was just a stay at home mom. None of my sisters or brothers had big careers we were just plain folks. When I was about five months I had no insurance and we had not gotten married yet I went to a doctor and he said your not pregnant you are just fat you need to go on a diet. I had not stopped having my monthly period I guess that is what he based his finding on I don't know. So I never went back to the doctor again until it was time to have my daughter God was good to me she was born healthy. Yes delivery pains were pains I knew nothing about and they were very bad, very, very. In the end I had a beautiful six-pound baby girl. And she was worth it all I went to live with my sister Lavonda and her family because it was best until I married Terri's father his name was Ted we got married before she was a year old, we rented a first floor apartment. With beautiful hard wood floor's, that I scrubbed on my hands and knee's.the owner would come by and said you could eat off my floors. We had a second child named Sherri this time we had insurance because he worked at American motors even then they paid good for a blue collar worker I'm not saying it was labor Ted was a loyal worker and worked hard. I was a stay at home mom our marriage had problems like all do Ted had a drinking and a ladies problem. Me I was insecure and we would fight something happen Ted went to jail I moved home again until I could get a job again. I really don't know why I can't remember what happen, for him to go to jail, I seem a chance to move out, without a fight and left. I got a job at a restaurant called Harvey's bought mom her first dinning room table big enough for all her family to set at. As she had been talking about for years. It was a long wooden table with twelve chairs I had everyone to keep her up stairs, until the store delivered. She said Earline what are you up to I know it is you? When she came down and seen it she just cried and smiled I really felt happy I had to pay on it weekly. I moved into a two-bedroom cottage behind a house. For a while when I first moved Ted started coming by to see the girls then he wanted to stay I would say no and he would try and fight. The police where called by me and he would leave before they came most of the time. I just didn't want to bring up my daughters that way. Finally he stopped fighting and we went to court for a divorce and child support. It was a little ugly because his family didn't want us to marry in the first place. I can understand now why because a parent wants the best as they see it for their children. I thank God it could have been a lot worse for us both I was not going to church or asking God for his guidance but God was always there as we know but sometimes we don't even think about how blessed we are. Once before I left Ted I remember going to the store for bread to fix his lunch for work I remember waking up in a snow bank, in my front yard.I could hear people talking and soon an ambulance came. And took me to the hospital, on the way he was taking my vitals and I heard him say she has no pulse. It scared me because I could hear them. Ted and I had a fight, and he hit me in the head with a bottle of alcohol. Because I had been talking to and yes was with a neighbor who happen to be white. We did like each other I had a concussion the doctors said and they told Ted to keep talking to me because if I went to sleep I might not wake up. So Ted kept talking and I came through it okay thank GOD Miracles how many can I have? I didn't see my friend any more after I left Ted. I had a friend named Maurice I don't remember how I meet him but we became good friends like brother and sister he would come by and see me and the girls often we would set and talk.he said he had a friend he wanted me to meet. When his friend gets out of jail. I said no thanks, but he told me he was a good guy. And I knew Maurice was, so I agreed to meet him. I can hear you now saying not again I have always wanted a husband and one that really loved me for me and one I could learn from and be my friend and I could do the same. And fill the same way not that I even knew how love was at that time in my life I don't think I really did. Well his friend did come home and he brought him over and we hit it off he of course was very nice looking to me but I was afraid of getting into a bad relationship again. Charles was and is his name he came over and we spent a lot of time together talking, he made clear if I really listen. That he didn't want a serious relationship. But I couldn't see the forest for the trees. I heard what I wanted to hear, that has been my problem, most of my life.I didn't want to see the negative, only the positive. Of all things but as we all know, it is not just one way. Again and again when I was hurt I would just bury it inside refuse to think about it at all, which is very dangerous. I always felt that if I loved someone enough they would love me back we all know that it does not work that way and for those of you that still don't. Please believe me. When I tell you save yourself a lot of pain. And pray and ask God for guidance, and patience to wait for him to send you your mate. I believe God has a mate for each one of his children if we would listen and be patience. God's time is not our time. And if you listen to the still small voice that speaks to us all you will not go wrong, there is no wrong in God, and God doesn't make mistakes. We would save ourselves a lot of pain and sorry. God does not use force; he has given us free will, his will, or our will. At the end of this book. I will have a list of scriptures, to back up what I believe by faith. At the end of the book for you, take it from someone, who has been there, more than once or twice, as I share, all I possibility can, remember with you. In hopes you will under stand with love, how I want to warn you, of some of the dangers of not living right. Sometimes we can see better, and hear clearer through someone else's trouble. And looking for the easy way out or around. and feeling like if you are not in control its not right. We must remember what God says revenge is mine, says the Lord. And we are no matches for getting revenge, the way God can. Remember he is our Creature, he made us He knows how many hairs we have on our head. Read the Holy Bible it will tell you. how can we have more knowledge of any kind than he can? And being insecure. I also want to share with you about doing it the right way. and share with you the joy of doing it the right way. I didn't until I had suffered like the children of the desert. Because of disobedience, until finally it soaked in. Gods way is the only right way, if you want peace, love, joy, and to be saved from all the suffering of disobedience. By the Grace of God I pray "Amen: this book is for all my sisters and brothers, all over the world. Life is so precious, and we should be careful not to use people. Life can be very fragile for all kinds of reasons. Charles said I have a great business head but common sense none I. Just in the last few years I hope I have gained a little. I am being a good daughter to my Heavenly Father and listening to him. And doing his will, His way. I didn't say I would not stumble. And fall but I know where to go. For what ever I need.to my Lord and savior Jesus. Charles and I spent weeks together night after night talking and getting to know each other we went out to the movies and dinner, one night after the movies we went by his parents house and they were very polite to me his family owned a bar. And I know very little about them, I don't think I fit in then or now. I always felt. Like I didn't fit in the family. You know like I was not good enough. And what really help me to look worse is that the police came out to their suburban home looking for me. about some stolen money orders that I had gotten from someone and cashed. And I would not tell them whom. They tried to scare me into telling where I got them. But I am not made like that. It was my choice, I used them to buy clothes for my children. And the store and police told the Judge. And that helped me a little got probation. This is Charles the first. All I can tell you is that he has two sisters and a brother. That's all I remember about his family. I believe it was my idea for him to start staying the night sometimes he wanted to go home but I would beg him to stay. Sometimes he would and sometimes not. I could fell a distance between us but you guessed it I hide the truth from myself. I was still working in restaurants doing some modeling for stores and I can sew naturally I made a lot of my own clothes. I was asked to make some clothes for a show. Starting with a tux and evening gown. Casual clothes for men and women, which I did I. didn't know where to take these talents. But I had them. I can even sing a little. I had no mentor, our guidance, no place that I knew of to go to. With these gifts. On my job as a waitress. I meet a man who told me I walked and acted like a natural dancer and he knew someone that had a club for strippers. Back then strippers couldn't touch their selves. Or make certain jesters. You were never fully undress when you took off your clothes you would have on what is now called a bikini when you striped. So I tried out for the club and became the club headliner Charles liked it. We were never allowed to set with the customers and the policewomen were always coming in with out notice. So I was good and protected from myself because I still had a nice mind yes I got flowers and offers of all kinds sometimes I was not sure what they wanted but was to ashamed to ask someone even my man. Well I got pregnant and had to stop working need I say Charles was not very happy.by this time he was staying most of the time with working and me when he could find work. I don't know why he did not find work with his family we never really talked about it. He would go out with friends at night a lot I didn't ask him what he was doing. I was just glad he was there when he was. Our handsome son was born looking just like his father except he had my freckles on his face Charles and I were both very olive complexion, the baby looked the same, my two daughters. Both have chocolate brown skin. Beautiful long black waved hair. Charles the third which we named him after his father and grandfather. Had curly thick black hair all of the children have small round faces.

I am blessed with beautiful children and I thank God for them. We continued to live together off and on for two years. With me saying we should be married, I always had enough sense to knew that it is wrong to live together. Even though I had never studied the bible. But I remember from going to Catholic school, and the teaching from the nuns, which were our teachers, when we lived in East Saint Louis Ill. This was the time of the unrest in Mil. There were problems coming to a head in Mil. There was talk of rioting; there was marching, and striking for and against civil rights. This happen in the mid sixties, Blacks, and Whites lived mixed in most of Mil. Even though we knew that our neighbor might not have liked us, we could live side by side until it seemed over night we as people Black and White, started to with draw I wanted out of this mess. After baby Charles was about twelve months I was pregnant again with our second child Charles was not ready for another child and his family also thought it was to soon. But what could I do I didn't believe in birth control or abortions. I had a hard time with this pregnancy mentally and physically I had a lot of pain and stayed in the hospital a lot in pain the baby's father would come to see me sometimes, but I was so insecure about him. That I was always crying and sad about how things were going, in our life together.I spent months, in the hospital before she was born. When she finally was born, she also was a beautiful baby. Lots of black weave hair, round face, brown in color and looked like a little Eskimo baby.all the nurses said she was so cute and was always holding her. When I took her home from the hospital Charles said he was leaving to go to Boston Mass. He had a friend there that could help him find work he couldn't find work in Mil. He said.I really got scared then he was leaving me with the children alone what was I going to do? Little did I know I was not alone if only I knew how turn to God I could have saved my self-a lot of pain and suffering. We need to learn that God knows all and can do all. nothing is to hard for him or to big or to small. If the hairs on our head were numbered by him he would have to know us all. He knows our enter most being our going in and our coming out he is our Creator he knows our all and all. He is never to busy or to tired, to sleepy. He is long suffering he never said I told you so. He treats us with perfect love. Perfection that is hard for us to understand. One thing I now know for sure he will never let you down if we could only trust in him. I can say these things now because I know now what I didn't know then. Charles left and he called me and kept in touch with me I started working toward getting the money to get to where he was. I worked hard to be ready when he was I was into white collar crime small one cashing stole money orders, being the pull man for soft shoe action I'm not proud of it but I did what I knew to do when I couldn't work on a regular job. About this time people were talking about riots so I pulled a small job and called the movers to come and pack I'm so glad God rains on the good and the bad he knows some of us didn't understand about our spirit on its way to hell. I called Charles and told him how much I had he said come on. We got out of there just in time yes I did wrong but I was not into hurting people or burning houses looting stores. Again I want to say this is about my life and the Grace of God and the Miracles he has done for me and to me. I don't want to through dirt on any one in order to tell my story. Charles was a hustler also and he knew that I would do some thing and sometimes we worked together. I was not into selling my body I was good at some con games, and could talk someone into giving up whatever I wanted. Because I was not a bad looking women. I could get a mans attention. What they usually wanted was sex. So it was a game, to see who could out con whom. I never gave it up not bragging just telling it like it was. The ladies always loved and was drawn to Charles a lot were what you call girls he had a few that showed him favor shall we say. Sometimes when they would get out of hand I would talk to them Charles also had a job as a lay counselor for a program. But kept his hustle on the side. Ladies were always calling the house for him.no I didn't like it, and we fought about it, but it didn't change.one day Charles got sick, and went into the hospital. And I was able to take over his job, until he could work again. One day driving home from work I seen his Cadillac in a drive way a few miles from the house of course everyone knew about this lady but me. I pull-up into the driveway, and it was on the fighting. xhe and I back and forth.he would come home, sometimes not. Finally he told me he loved her. And left me and the kids. I cried for so long time my eyes closed swollen shut. A friend from my job came by, because no one had heard from me in a few days, and found me in a breakdown, of none function. I was in such bad shape.he took the kids to his house. And call the ambulance, to take me to the hospital. First they put me in the physic ward. Then after I talked to the doctor he said my problems were real. And let me out of the hospital.I want home there was no money in the bank. it was all gone.to be fair at one point in our marriage I meet someone, and I told him.I was not going to have an afraid. He called Charles and told him that he loved me and wanted to take care of the children and me. Charles said he respected me for that and he was going to do better never happen for us and I didn't have an affair I didn't see or talk to him again. I was never unfaithful in our marriage God is my witness. Things were hard for a while but by the Grace of God I got stronger and tried to make a home for the kids and me. I stayed in Springfield for a while longer. I kept having very bad headaches and kept going to the emergency room one day I over heard a doctor say I was just lonely I was very mad lonely I was not of all things not with all the kids I had. So when I went back the next time, the doctor gave me the name of a specialist.I was in his office for less than a half an hour.he said I had a bone pressing on a nerve, in my head and forming a tumor. And that I needed sugary right away. He said I would need someone to take care of the children that it would be a while before I could do it. I called the two oldest grandmothers and she said she would help me and I sent them on a plane to Mil. The stewardess watched them I explained to the girls want was wrong with me and that I loved them and soon as I was strong enough I would come and get them. I explained all this to the grandmother and told her I would be calling the girls the girls were eight and six I cried when they left because I was not sure if I was going to live or die. The doctor said I could be blind, paralyzed or die and I needed to be in a good frame of mind before he would operate. He ask me was I alone? Did I have someone to be with me? I told him no.he called my mother, and she told him she couldn't make it. I told him I would be fine, Charles kept the two younger kids his kids, he, and his new wife, I didn't like the idea, but I didn't tell the kids. I had the surgery and was blessed to come out fine another Miracle thank God. It was a long time to recuperate I would call the girls after a while, their grandmother didn't want to give them back.I understand now, but then I was very angry. I had to go to court and fight hard to get them back. The judge gave them back after I had kept letters and phone bills to verify that I was constantly in touch. Which didn't make the grandmother happy. I had to fight the court in Mil. By then I was married again ask me why but thank God I was it was better for me my lawyer said. After the case was over my new husband decided to go into the army and he was transfer over seas. We were very unhappy but we couldn't do any thing about it. So he went and we made plans to follow him later after he got orders for us to come over. In the mean time we stayed in Mil. All the kids and I was happy because I got a chance to see mom and most of my siblings who were scattered all over the states, I was happy to see the ones near. I tried to find a job and start saving but I had no luck I was always getting sick with kidney infections and blather infections the doctor said I needed a cystascope. It is an operation were they but a tube in your blather and let all the water out because it was not happening naturally. After that I wanted to loose some weight.so I took diet pills. Not a smart move, I was not eating proper, I begun to feel very weak. It seemed like my life was leaving me. I could not walk. God gave me strength to call out. And one night I crawl to the back door and called for the lady up stairs in her apartment to please come and help me. She thank God, she called her mother, who came right over. The Doctor told me later, at the hospital. That I probably had at least one heart attack earlier that day. And didn't realize it. and they carried me to the hospital in her car. When I got there, the doctors told me I was very sick, ask me if I wanted them to contact my family? I said no, they told me I was in very bad shape that my heart was very weak. That I may die. I still said no, then the lady that came with me told me it would be best so I did I just didn't want to worry my family. I remember my family coming. And my mother crying.I was in and out of it most of the time.I was on very strong medicine. One of my brothers that were male nurse changed hospitals so he could be near me. It helped a little the army wouldn't let my husband come home at first finally they did after a lot of paper work. Again God blessed and I got better my husband went back over seas. By this time I was very depressed I just didn't know which way to turn. One day a young white man came to my door I was very hostile to him he was very nice and ask me if the family wanted to go to bible school around the corner at the Lutheran church I said no and that I didn't believe in GOD! He said we'll can the children come I said no he said he would be back and he was going to pray for me.I don't think I really meant it I was just scared and angry lonely and didn't know what to do or how to ask for help. I believe the man did pray for my family and me. One night the kids and I were in the bed and I heard a window break next thing I knew the house was in flame. We all got out safely thank God and my oldest daughter Terri told the next door neighbor that if I had a Pepsi I would feel better. I'm standing in three feet of snow. In the dead of winter, with no shoes on, and hear comes my baby with a Pepsi. And said I hope you feel better.I felt all-warm in side. After the fire nothing was left we lost every thing thank God for Insurance HOW MANY MIRACLES CAN I HAVE? We all stayed with mom I decided to take the insurance money and go to my husband in Japan with all the children.the Red Cross called my husband. And he called me, and said he would get orders for us to come. We had to get shots, and pass ports for all.I was finally happy for a while.oh I for got to tell you, when I went back into the house, after the fire it was so hot glass melted. Around my bed where I slept with my son that night smoke was all around but didn't come near the bed like a shield was around the bed God is my witness its true. I wanted to do something nice for mom before I left so I sent her to the beauty collage were one of my siblings worked name Vicki to get a complete from head to toe, while she was there someone said something to my mom disrespectful.to her. Some one called me. And told me what happen. I went down town in a cab, with my husband's gun. And by the time I got there, everyone was gone. The door was open, and no one was insight I mean In the whole Beauty School. I could only find the security guard and I let him have it he found the owner of the beauty school and she apologized to my mom and me. You know I was like a walking time bomb full of pain it didn't take much for me to explode thank God he was with me in my hell or I would have been lost. Finally we got our orders to leave we got on the plane and except for a stop in Canada which was roped we couldn't leave a restricted area we were on the plane about twenty six hours, and finally we landed in Tokyo. And had to spend the night, at the Imperial hotel, because the Japanese police ask me if I had anything to declare. I said yes, a gun that was my husbands. And that I had told the airlines and it was apart in my luggage. It was not loaded. And it was taken apart. They went crazy I didn't speak the language and no one spoke English. I was really scared here I was standing in a foreign country airport with four children, on my way to jail. If I couldn't explain, that this gun was my husbands and he was in Okinawa, in the army. And I am bringing it to him. Someway I got the message across to them thank God. But we missed our plane so we had to stay at the Imperial hotel in Tokyo for the night. I was very tired and of course the kids were to and hungry so I picked up the phone and tried to get some food for us and everything was closed. On the way up to our room the bell hop said Jackson five family I believe only because my son had a very big afro I laugh and said no at that time I could have used some of the Jackson s money mine was getting very slim. But we got a good rest, and the next morning boarded a plane for the rock, which is Okinawa. When we landed it seemed as if we landed, in the middle of the water. On a patch of land.I was scared, and I could not see my husband anywhere. Finally I seem him, I didn't show him how, and glad I was to see him, until later. I cried, and laughed and he held me. And said every thing would be all right, I really needed to hear that. God knew I did. Most of my life, that is some thing that I didn't hear enough. That everything would be all right, No one cared enough, to give me what I needed. Such simple words, Which have a very powerful meaning, and can, change a life just to hear. You didn't even have to love me, to say them just care enough about a life in general. I was so excited, and scared and tired. But I believe my actions showed him later on. Later that night at the hotel, when the children were sleeping. We stayed at the motel, until we could find an apartment. His rank didn't come through, like he hoped for. For base housing. So we were going to have to live off base for a while he said. We finally found a small house and moved in with only our clothes again God continued to bless us some how he got us beds to sleep on and a hot plate and electric skillet you would be surprise how inventive you become when you have to. We started to learn a little of the language just from our neighbors which were nice we watched the school kids go back and forth to school they spent long hours in school our kids went to school on base which was Fort Buckner. We shopped on base for everything because it was cheaper. This was when the Yen was between two and three hundred per dollar which would buy you a loaf of bread off base or a coke. I got a job working on base for a while. Then they cut back and said we would be called back later. But here we go again I got pregnant surprise! This time the doctor said I had to have an abortion. Because my heart was too weak, it would not stand me, carrying and giving birth. He bluntly told me I was going to die. He seemed so distant and cold, no nice words no hope, just prepare your family, make arrangement for your children, just like that.I was put in the hospital and they ran test after test I said no I would not have an abortion. And he said be prepared to die. I was so afraid and confused. I cried and cried I, took an overdose of pills. And they rushed me back to the hospital again. But I think I was just asking for help.I was really lost inside and scared, I felt like I was all alone in the world never felt like I could count on any one but my self. When I would ask for help no one would or could, or seem to care, my life didn't seem to be valuable to any one, unless they needed something from me. I am not feeling sorry for my self, even as a child not even my birthdays were celebrated or even acknowledge. God is my witness I am just stating a fact.I was always willing, to help any one any time.I didn't and dont know any other way to be I get a good feeling just by helping. The doctor also said I was having twins I was sent back to the states on a hospital plane. I was suppose to lay in the bed on the plane, all the way back to the states. I didn't I got up and smoked. And they would say you must lay down your heart needs rest, but I fought back. While I was in the hospital before we left the rock that's what we called Okinawa. A young lady came to see me, she ask me did I want her to pray for me. I don't know if she was an angel or not I answered yes, she ask me if I new Jesus.I said no, she said she would come, back if she could, I thanked her and I never saw her again. All I can remember is that she had on a uniform. I was taken to Great Lakes Navel hospital and then on a regular flight to Mil. I stayed with mom until I could get an apartment for the kids and I., which my husband bought, back on a civilian plane. My mom brought me my first birthday cake. And my brother Forthune, bought me one. And a present, I had never received a cake, or celebrated with the family before my birthday. I have no idea why it was never done. I knew I was dying, then so the kids and I moved into, and apartment after a while, my husband came back again, because when he brought the kids home he couldn't stay. He tried to get a hardship home, but the army said no. He had to go back before the babies were born. My brother Tony came by and would spend the night sometime my sister Lavonda who lived a block away with her husband and family and still lives there it's a big beautiful house they own. My husband told Terri my oldest that he was not coming back he didn't let me know before he left. The night I went into labor my brother was there so I went to the hospital alone and my daughter was born healthy and with no complications How Many Miracles Can I Have. She was not a twin but a very good and healthy child; my oldest daughter told me that my husband had made some improper advances to her. She was only about eleven. I was hurt and mad, at first I thought she was saying he raped her but he just said something to her. I didn't want to say this in the book because I don't want to hurt our daughter that we have together but I fell like it needed to be said. Not that she had anything to do with it but it is her dad. Well need I say I just stuffed the pain and confusion away with the mountains of other pain and fear? And tried to go on with stumbling through life trying to be the best mom I could I have always loved my children and wanted them to love me back. I always did what ever I had to do,so that they could have what was needed. Which was growing up with a father. And some of what they wanted, I had a friend named Dee, she introduces me to someone, I liked him, I wanted a father for my children. Oh by the way I hurried up and got a divorce from the man I was married to. Then my friend Dee introduced me to a man name Charles I just wanted someone who would love us.

l believed that it was possible to find someone.I don't know how I could still believe but I did. I found out that he was a schoolteacher and some times a sub principle he was also not a slick person. He was not trying to get over on me to get in my bed or looking for a free ride. I didn't want to get into any of that again also I watched him around my daughters and my son and would talk to my children about him how they felt about him and was he nice when I was not around? They liked him, and never wanted him to go home. But you see he had to go home sometimes, he was married. Yes I did want a nice guy, someone special. And I didn't know the first thing about how to allow one in my life, I didn't know what to look for, I always lead with my heart, not my head. Not even asking for Gods help, which is exactly what I needed. He told me that he was not happy and that working two jobs she would not even fix him dinner he said he caught her with someone I know now that two wrongs don't make a right.we decided to leave town together and start over again. So we left and moved to Denver together.we hardly had any money. And when we got ready to leave for Denver I backed up my station wagon to his back yard. Like he told me to and moved him out. And his wife and her friend stood in the window I could have been shot are hurt boy was I dumb. But God loved and still love me inspire of the mess I get into. God, is a problem solving, long suffering God. Who loves his children with a perfect love that we can't even comprehend? God is a long-suffering God and Mercy full to his children and I am here to tell you that if it was not for him I would have been dead and buried and in hell. Thank God for his love, the more I learn of God the more I love him. None can love, us liked he does. Who do you know, that would love you knowing, that you would deny him, and would be disobedient. But still chose you, while you were yet in your mother womb. And even before and yet gave us free will to live his way or, stumble through life with not, even giving him the praise, for the gift of life or the blessing, he gives us along the way. That only he can give, and as he continue s to bless you.to live and get you out of one mess or another time and time again oh praise the Lord! When we are in trouble than we call on him. Bless his name, He shed his blood, God gave his only begotten son to be born and suffer and to die, that we may have the gift of forgiveness of our sins, and to let us know that we can live a holy life, Christ being the perfect example. We think we know what love is only God knows the true meaning of love OH PRAISE HIS NAME! What a wonder he is today yesterday today and tomorrow. When we got to Denver we ran across a mailman who owned some apartments and rented us one a one bedroom. We ran out of money and the kids had to eat Charles was trying to get his paper work in order so he could work by sub teaching which took a while so I got a job at Mc Donald but it was going to take two weeks to get paid so I went to Safeway and ask to see the manager he came over and I told him that I had just come to Denver with my five children and was trying to get settled and that I had found a job at McDonald but it would be two weeks before I would get paid and I was out of money, and my kids were hungry,and I was not going to steal.he called the security guard over, and together they had about seven dollars.I said thank you,and I would give it back to them.he said that's okay, and after I shopped. Thank God for chicken. I went home, and cook for my family. I told Charles what I had done. He seemed shocked but what could I have done? He gave me a card, with the name of the employment office, of Safeway on it and told me to go, apply for a job and I did, and was hired. My next door neighbor worked at Safeway also one day we were standing outside talking and I was telling her about how glad I would be, when we got paid. And that it was a tight squeeze, right now.she said how much do you need? I said no that's okay. She said I would help you. How much is a couple hundred okay? Will that help? I didn't know what to say.I was in shock, didn't believe it, until she called over a day or two later and handed it to me. Tell me again how good God is. She moved and bought herself and her children a home. She has three children I believe. We moved into a larger apartment that the mail- man owned after he came by while Charles and I was gone and seen how well behaved the children acted. And how clean I keep the apartment. With five children and two adults. Living in such a small place. He told us this later, after he offered us a new place. Was a two bedroom, and nice by then Charles was working teaching as a sub, English teacher, he knew I didn't have much education.I only had two weeks, of the eighth grade. I had told him once, that I wanted to be a teacher. He said you can if you want to I didn't think I was good enough.so he started working with me and the book that you can study to get ready for the test I would get so mad and fuss the kids would just laugh at me. Yes God did it again and between God and he using Charles.I got my ged and the same day applied for entrance to college. I went for financial aid, and the head of the financial aid office, said you cant make it here, with just the education you have. He said I needed more of a formal education. He said I needed more of basic education. From grade school and High school. That's all I needed to hear. That was my best year In collage a 3.5 gpa. with and English major and Black Studies, as my minor. Then Charles started acting strange, and the medicine he was being sent buy his mother was late coming. So I took the jar that it came in and took it to the health center.the lady looked at me and sent me up stairs to the mental health clinic. Little did I know that Charles was a schizophrenic? I didn't understand until the doctor told me that my husband was very sick we had gotten our divorces and gotten married. He asks me if I called my husband, would he come to the clinic? I said yes, he said are you sure. I called Charles and he came. Together we learned that he was a schizophrenic. and needed this medicine to function he had been told for many years that it was for his stomach by his family. It was hard to work now because he was going through crisis over and over and wanted to kill his self and me I was still going to school and working part time. It really got bad so I called Vicki one of my sibling and she came out to Denver to help me out. She stayed with us for a while, I really was glad for the help. Thank God for the Ram in the bush. We got housing help, from the government, In paying our rent, because Charles was not able to work any more. But he was doing much better, and Vicki my next to the youngest sibling went back and forth between Mil. And Denver we found a beautiful home and moved in by then I was doing my student teaching I didn't have a baby setter because Charles went to school with me and would set in the car, until I finish my classes, he would do okay, but some times I would keep Terri or Sherri, home from school, if I had and exam, and Charles was not well enough, to keep the baby, there was no child care help for me, I know that It was against the law, but I felt like I didn't have a choice. I was going to school, to better my self for my children and my self. One day I spanked Terri and Sherri and when they went back to school some how I don't want to blame anyone the police were called and the girls were taken to a shelter I had spanked them with a switch from a tree and they had marks on their legs they came to my home and found it very nice and my lawyer who happen to have been to my home on more than one occasion our minister had been to my home and had been around my children and knew me and Charles both Terri told them on her own that she deserved a spanking. I was told that my other daughter said I would beat her with a lead pipe until I blackout,that hurt more than anything, God in heaven,knows that never happen, but the more I tried, to get her to come home, the worse she acted, finally she told them, that she didn't want to see me, It was very painful for me, that I had a child that didn't want, to be at home, The last thing I ever wanted, was for my child, not to be home, I begged and pleaded with her, she acted worse, the worse it got the more lost I felt, I called my sister to come, from Calif. she came, and even told Sherri, that she could come, and stay with her.she didn't want that ether, she wanted to be on her own she was only 13 yrs old. I know I was very strike with boys and dating. But I was not that bad I pray. So she was taken away I felt lost I stopped going to school and came out to Oakland to see my sister and go hooked on it. I wanted to move away from the pain that I was in.so helpless about I tried to keep in touch with my daughter, but was told she wanted nothing to do with me. I was told by the Social Workers that my daughter said I beat her with A lead pipe. God in Heaven I could never do any think like that to anyone. Especially a child my child. So we packed up and moved this time by moving van and off to Oakland we came.I told social services were we lived and phone number if she wanted to talk or see us. Just for the record God in heaven knows I would never hit any child! Someone or mine ease with a led pipe or any thing like. After that I was afraid to even punish my children. Even with a time out I was scared.I didn't want to loose them this went on for years.the youngest one I never touched And to this day she does not speak to me unless I can do something for her it hurts my heart. The older ones I had but mostly punish them by no television or stay in their room. Charles got worse again and I sent him home to stay with his family. for years I had taken care of him I needed a break while he was away I meet someone. Who happen to be a you, guessed it a hustler and he had his own detail shop for cars. Charles came back but he was still sick and going through a crisis. I sent him back home and was seeing we will call him cap. He had a truck and a couple of cars none were new. I didn't think anything about how much money he had. He was good to me he gave me at least a diamond a day flowers people would come with whatever they had to sell and if I wanted it was mine yes there were plenty of other women in his life but he came home with me every. He had a wife but it was years since they were together he had children by his wife and other women he took care of them all I bought a house nothing fancy and worked. Went back to school but had to quit the kids needed me home, so I worked at different jobs some good some not so good but I liked to work and earn money. I remember soon as we moved into the house I had locked the kids bikes into the garage with a very large lock and we left and when we came back the bikes were stolen.I called the police he ask me how long had I been in the neighborhood /. I said I just bought the house he said it was a bad idea he said if I could get out to do so its not a good area. I didn't understand then I went around the neighborhood looking for the bikes I found them right on the corner the kids said they got them from somebody I said they were mine and called the police. And got them back, the house where the kids lived on the corner was a dope house. Heroin was the drug of choice it seemed. Flash back while I was still living in the apartment one of the apartment managers relative that was seeing one of the tenants who seemed to have a thing for men about fifteen years her junior.two of her boyfriends got into a fight.one was a security guard in uniform, that evening it was about six or seven. The security guard had a gun and handcuffs. He handcuffs the other man and pushed him up against the wall. While we all looked on helpless while he beat him. We called the police and told them what was going on.we screamed at the man to stop and told him we called the police. He pushed the man up against the wall, after the man seem to be semi concise he shot him in the back of the head and killed him. It was about five or six witness's and the man said you didn't see anything did you talking to us as the other man lay dead on the ground by the pool.the police did come. Took our statements and arrested the man. I believe he was charged with manslaughter.we were never asked to come to court. That was the first time I had seen someone killed. My God it was a horrible sight I will never forget it. I had moved into the house before the deal closed.I wanted out of that place after the murder. I mean I wanted out of the apartment, Before I moved cap and I went shopping. Cap was my boyfriend Cap was his nick name. We went to a jewelry store were they knew him very well. He was treated like a very good customer. And I was treated like I was Mrs. Cap. He started giving me a diamond a day, and more some times. Always a good size one I started taking them to the jewelry store.to one of the daughters named Susie.she was very good to me and cap we both had excellent designs. I would buy a ring or something already made sometimes. I had jewelry made for cap to with diamonds he gave me. He told me his product was coming up short mostly his coke. He sold coke and weed he wanted me to set at the apartment were his products were sold and watch I begin to ask questions about how you weight it and how you cut the drug and with what do you cut it? Caps cousin got me a book on how to cut cocaine. And with that the more I learned the more I took over cutting and packaging the cocaine. Did it ever acure to me what I was doing. I have no idea what a hell hole I was digging for myself. He was so good to me better than I had felt about myself I finally had someone to lean on. I just wanted to make him happy I didn't know how to tell him no. That I could go to jail just didn't think about it. Excited about the money and how it grew business was booming cap was happy. Then one night he came home with some cocaine and said did I want to try it I was scared but he told me he was with me and I did. That started my life of drug use I started out every morning with tooting coke. Then after a while of these, he told me about acid paper acid. Then it was coke and acid and brandy in the morning before and while I showered in the morning and got dressed for my day then came the introduction to free base I never had to pay for it so no warning about how much I was spending on it. Before I closed the deal on the house I became very ill with my lungs filled with fluids you guessed it pneumonia. I was in intensive care when the loan officer came to the hospital with the good news that I was given the loan for the house. God blessed me to get better and I went home and closed the deal on the house. I kept my kids away from my life style all business was done at the apartment of caps they just enjoyed all the things money got for them they were spoiled. When cap would come home he would bring things like gallons of milk and boxes of steak for the kids I had met a lady whom happen to be a policewomen. Who lived under me when I lived at the apartments. She and I were the same when it came to punishment for our teens. Our sons were about the same and one of my daughters they were the same age. just like kids they got into everything together nothing bad.we became very good friends I think we exchanged gold and diamonds during the holiday. We went out to clubs together and had a good time.we both just sort of sat and looked at the people. I took her to my jewelry's and introduced her.

She became a good customer to. People called us the crook and the cop. cap told m e he was taking me to Louisiana with him I was so happy some of his family lived down there and he was going to bring back his grandfather for a visit to Calif. So I made arrangement for someone to stay with the kids while we were gone. Before we left I got a call from my stepfather he and I were friends he called to tell me he had cancer he was crying. I flew home to Mil to see him and ask mom why didn't they come out here? I could help to take care of them better. And while we were in Louisiana they moved next door to me. When we came back they were already moved in. we had a great time down south. Every where we went his family feed us and feed us very well. We had fresh vegetables corn bread with the best pot liquor you ever had fresh fried fish. Sweet potato pie fresh yams my favorite fried chicken and fresh buttermilk that you could later for a bedtime snack put your corn bread in and eat to your hearts content. His grandmother had me laughing so hard.she said when cap and I pulled up in the car, she said she thought I was white. And said Lord has mercy my baby has brought a white woman down. She saw my blonde hair and fair complexion. Cap was a chocolate a dark chocolate brown and I was fair we matched very well I thought. When I wash my hair she said I looked like a plucked chicken.I tried to explain to her, she said it was not the perm. I just laughed we didn't get a chance to do any sight seeing cap was busy selling drugs and hanging out with his friends and I enjoyed hanging with his family and grandmother and walking to the country store. I was treated very well by all he took me around to meet his family some lived out in the country. He took me out to his uncles home and farm It was beautiful His uncle ask me if I was afraid to feed the hogs and did I know how I said no I was not afraid and I do know how to feed them.

His uncle gave me some boots and a bucket of food for the hogs and out I went and feed them. They laughed because they though I was just a fancy city girl. I guess he wanted to see how I would act. Before we left Oakland cap told me not to bring a lot of fancy clothes. But of course I didn't listen to him. I did bring a pair of jeans and I cut them off. That with a shirt is all I wore most of the time. When it was time to go I didn't want to go cap was tired so I said I would drive first I like driving the Lincoln. I put some crank in my coffee. Oh I forgot to tell you that I had added crank to my list of drugs.I drove all the way back to Oakland.his grandfather ask? Are you tired I said no, little did cap known that I had taken all but a small amount I started with a rock the size of an apple when I finished it was the size of a peach seed. He told me to hold and used it. When we got to Oakland it was very little left I didn't care he had always given me my way. Cap went back to seeing the ladies he would stay out more and we had a argument and broke up we went back and forth I still had my way we stayed friends. I would run around the lake and pick up packages for him and would go where he ask me.I got to know some of the places to go and pick up drugs. At first they didn't like it but he said if they wanted to do business they would have to deal with me so they did. One day cap called me at home and said he was going to get a stingray I said I wanted min e first he laughed later on that night I called him because I didn't hear from him all day. Some strange mans voice answered the phone I ask were cap he said he's not here I said who are you he said a friend I said were is he? He said he was outside I sad let me speak to him he said he cant come to the phone I said I don't believe you I'm on my way over their. When I got there one of his people met me in the driveway and told me cap was dead and that the police was up in the apartment going through everything, I was in shock I just walked around the pool. Someone told me it was not safe and that I should leave. I seen a car come in the back way, and a man got out, and went into his trunk. I got a little scared but I kept walking around the pool he got back into his car and left when I look back now what a nut I was I was in so much pain added to all the other pain I hadn't gotten rid of. Then my husband showed up at my door the kids were glad to see him I was just numb it was expected of me to take care of the arrangement for the funeral. I ask his wife she said she knew I was his woman. Whatever I wanted to do was okay with her.so I had his favorite white suit that I had gotten him. His family came from out of town and some stayed with me I told Charles I owed cap at least this much he took very good care of the children they wanted for nothing. And to please stay in the bedroom while the family was there. He did as I ask him and stayed in the room, I know that it hurt him but I had to do this for Cap. It was really hard to do, all went well if a funeral can go well and his family left. Charles left again this time because his father was Ill and he was needed to be with family. I went to work for a home improvement company, as phone solicitors. Learning the business from the ground up. Soon I was the office manager. I had about eight phone solicitors working for me and the salesmen coming in for the leads for home improvement jobs I notice that the prices were high for the jobs that was being done. I over heard a lot of conversion from salesmen and I started asking questions and getting to know who the vendors were that we did business with. Complaints started coming in and all of a sudden the company closed down. I was very angry because they owed me money. But I got an Idea from a friend that I had meet a salesman in the business and I got a contractor to allow us to work under his license number and we formed our own company.my son and I worked together doing hot tar and gravel roof. Also I had a friend whose father needed a two room, lad built inside of a warehouse. And he paid me seven thousand to do the job. I Sub contracted out the framing and electric work. All the rest we did I had about six men working with me. Other businesses came in to see this being done. They didn't think I could do the job. But I did the job and the customer was very pleased and we were on schedule. One of my employees and I were seeing each other and he wanted it to be more serious and he wanted to be my man I said no and I was going to stop seeing him all together. He didn't like that.One evening after working all day I fell asleep on the sofa while we were talking. I kept a 25-caliber handgun in my purse he took it from my purse while I was half a sleep. And ran out side I woke up as he was leaving and I went to the living room window to see what he was up to and he pointed the gun at the window and fired. I turned and ran through the house.I didn't want to scream or make any noise because the kids were asleep.I ran to the back door as I reached for the door knob it fell off into my hand. In the dark I reached down and picked it up and open the door. And ran outside and around the house as he continued to shoot. And around the front of the apartments were my mothers and step dad lived. And around to the back and ended up on the other side of moms apartment building. Into a dead end, it was my fence and it was eight feet high, just then I fell to the ground, and said to my self that if he shoots, it will be in my back, just then someone open a window in moms apartment building. And said man don't do it.I just got out of the pen, for the same thing. Its not worth it, I'm laying face down eating dirt. Funny but I was not scared just mad. That's all I heard the man say. Then I heard my moms voice say son, you better drop it, and my step dad say if you finger looks like it may move, you are dead. So put the gun down slowly son. He drop the gun the police came, He went to jail then I got scared and crying and had to go to bed under the doctors care. He called me from jail and pleaded with me. And said he was sorry, and that he would go to the pen, if I didn't drop the charges. Dropped the charges, and the judge made me pay court cost. I told him if he was ever seen around, I would have him recharged. He left and I didn't hear from him again. And just when I thought things were settling down my son was skipping school and the kids were not getting the things that they had when cap was alive.my son started hanging out around the corner. And people would tell me I would go and pick him up and bring him home. Or take him back to school he kept doing it. This went on and on finally one day a kid on a bike came over to the house and said that the housing authority police had arrested Charlie with a lot of other boys and had him in a car handcuffed. I rushed around there and ask them what did they think they were doing with my son in that car? They said he was selling drugs and was under arrest. I told him that he was a lie in no uncertain terms. And took my son out of the car. They kept picking him up and I kept getting him out finally one day I came around the corner mad and fussing at the housing police and a young man on a bike called me Mama Soul.I said why are you calling me that? He laughed and said that is your name. His name was ray that name stuck like glue and spread like a wild fire so when there was a fight or the police was bothering the boys they called me Mama Soul and would tell me what ever was going on and ask for my help. During this time Charles came back his father had died. Then we had another visitor Charles the first one I married came to visit. Charles the second was very upset, about his visit. But as I told him he is the father of two of my children. And he has a right to see them.I was glad he came In a way, I was hoping that he could sway our son, from hanging with the people he was. And concentrate on school. My son Charles was on the track team, and was very good.he had been written up in the paper several times. They said he could be another Renaldo Neiromoa.I tried to encourage him to stick with it. But I was so busy taking care of home, and trying to satisfy Charles, the second and keep peace. That I didn't do enough for my son, I didn't go to his track meets. Like I should have. I didn't know how important it was for me to be there at the meet with him. Yes I encouraged him but he needed more from me. I always felt so burden down with the problems and pain and responsibly I had because I had to be father and mother and nurse to my husband. Along with trying to be a loving mother, and father to the children, and patient with them all. But Charles was a good son to me he and my daughters brought me lots of joy and love when they were young. As my daughters came to the age of thirteen one by one they drew away from me except for my oldest she was closer than my other daughters did and still is. She never totally turned against me as my others have done and still do. God only knows why, I pray I was never that bad a parent. Back to the visit from Charles the first, while he was here we were invited to SanJose to a ministers home. A man that I had known in the world but had gave his life to Christ. The same one that got me the job of building the lab for his father.He invited my whole household and visitor to come. Charles the second would not come but Charles the first and all four children came.At his home I received Jesus as my Lord and savior and we all prayed and I thank God for given me the will to go. After that I started going to a church in Oakland along with prayer and bible study with the Minister from San Jose when he would come down to Oakland or I would go to his home. The more I learned, about how God loved me, the more I wanted to learn. Then I meet some prayer warriors. And started running for my life, the more I went with them, to churches to pray.the more I wanted to go, I was seeking the Baptism of the Holy Ghost, that comforter I needed, that staying power that I had heard about. I would go to noonday prayer and go with the prayer warriors. Then One night I was so tired and when the lady one of the praying women called to see if I was going I said I was so tired. She said I should press my way and go, that God would bless me.so I did and we went to a store front church, and very simple it had very little I said I could have stayed home to my self. Little did I know what god had in store for me? I had no Idea what It was like, to receive the Baptism of the Holy Spirit. But as began to pray my tongue started to quiver and I started to lose control of my tongue. I was Baptize in the Holy spirit with evidence speaking in tongues was so happy I wanted to tell the world that It really happens Then it was prophesied to me that I was a Missionary and that God would reveal to me what kind. II kept going to prayer, and going to church with my kids, and Charles the second when he would go.One day I went to noon day prayer, as I was getting down on my knees to pray. A voice spoke to me, and said Evangelist.I have never heard, a voice like that, In my life. It was a feeling of almighty power and such over powdering love, and strong as great thunder. Going off in my head. Great power very hard to under stand, in a voice like no other. It's very true when God says my children know my voice, and that's not an execration. Then the lord sent my daughter the second oldest that I had not seen since she was about thirteen, when she left home. And she was saved thank God, and was on her way to Germany, to marry her fiancée. But while she was home, we enjoyed the Lord together, with the rest of my family.my son started going less and less like his step dad. But at night all the girls and sometimes my son, would sleep in my room. Some on the floor, some in my bed, one morning Sherri my second child, said she seen the number seven, and Jesus standing, at the head of my bed, over me.. I felt so blessed, and very humble, to be so honored.One day I was telling my son, how God was blessing us. And that I wanted him to go to church more. And why didn't he want to go? Finally my son told me, the truth that he was selling drugs. I was hurt and scared for him and he said he would leave home I didn't want him to leave home. I went to the pastor, and told him what I was dealing with. And told him, how troubled I felt. And how lost I felt. That I felt like I should leave the church, because of my sons life style. And that I didn't want him to leave home. Little did I know that I would be putting my son before God if I left? But the Pastor didn't tell me what I should do. Or that I would be putting my son, over God and how wrong It would be. He didn't tell me to seek God In prayer really didn't get the help, that I was looking for or needed. I ended up getting into the business my self of selling weed with and for him My God what a terrible mistake to add to all the other mistakes I made. But God knows that I didn't understand what I was doing and didn't under stand that all I had to do was seek him for the help I needed, and know one made it clear to me when I reached out for help. I can imagine what some of you think of me already but I'm going to tell you the whole truth maybe it will help someone from making Some of the same mistakes we have. To step up to the plate and tell it like it is. For all the kids and families out there and let them know that there is a way out. And no matter how bad those things get or how deep you are in you can get out nothing is to hard or to complicate for God He can do all things if you just let him. A surprise came one summer little Charles natural father came to Oakland for a few weeks one summer I had told him what our son was doing. He stayed about a week and left after that I got deeper and deeper I started helping the boys become more business Before I got in to selling drugs with my son I was invited to a friends house with my sons father for prayer.we went with the children.my sons father and I excepted Jesus as our personal savior.I gave up cigarettes and drinking, and drugs no one believed me but I did. My husband didn't believe me because daily I called him all kinds of mfs. Plus that was just my way.I treated him like a dog.he never complained but when I gave my life to Jesus he said he missed being called the dirty names.I felt bad that I had treated him like that. I started going to church and to prayer every day seeking the Holy Ghost and seeking more of God. I would go with the prayer warriors to pray where ever they went making clothes for a couple of lady Evangelist for revivals I was running for my life as fast as I could. One night I went with the prayer warriors to a little storefront church they said they had been ask to come and pray. So we went I looked at this broken down church with the floor squeaking and the old piano off key. I was so tired from going to churches and praying and seeking the baptism of the Holy Spirit.I k new in my spirit that I needed it. I long for it I needed the staying power. As we got down on our knees to be began praying I began to say thank you Lord. And the more I said it I could feel something happening to my tongue. Like I had no control of it and an utterance came. And I receive my Baptism of the Holy Spirit.I did nothing but just praise the Lord I wanted to scream out loud but I didn't. I open my eyes to see what the prayer worriers were doing they were praying and giving thanks for the Precious Blood of the Lamb. After prayer was over I hurried and told them what had happen to me and they said God had given me my Baptism of the Holy Spirit I was so happy they said just keep seeking him praise him more and more. And I did I went to prayer wherever I knew it was going on. And my tongues became more and more strong. Some times I would ask the Lord what language was he and I speaking would answer Indian, Jewish Arabic etc. God is so great what a mighty God we serve. I just stopped in the middle of writing and called a friend and we had prayer God came in and Blessed our souls and said Miracles on today I am excited for I believe I walk by faith and not by sight. Every day I would fast until I come back from prayer because I believe if you deny the flesh just for God he will honor it and come closer to you in your spirit. I love the feeling of the presence of the spirit of the living God. One evening a friend came from San Jose and brought some people with him my kids and I was having bible study all but my son he was doing his thing. Hanging out with his friends and selling drugs or seeing one of his girlfriends. Don't get me wrong he was my best friend and a good son the best son. I just didn't know how to reach him I went to church with him and my daughters talk to him about good and evil I just couldn't reach him I was afraid of loosing him so I didn't push hard enough. Back to the bible study when my friends came we greeted each other and had prayer. There was a women setting in a dining room chair and the spirit spoke and said go pray for her and I did she just went to what seems like sleeping in the chair she didn't fall out or lean over her head was bowed and she was slain in the spirit we call it God sent me from one to the other until all was slain no the floor in the chairs on the couch my youngest daughter was going around covering the ladies with whatever she could find.so that their bodies were covered.my oldest daughter was watching and laughing. I told her to stop and to pray because any demons that came out of any one could come into them if they were not praying. She started praying and I went over to her. As I was lead and all of a sudden a loud howl came out of her like a hurt animal. God is my witness then I went over to my second oldest daughter.yes she was home she came home on her way to Germany to wed her finance. I went over to pray for her and her body lifted up off the sofa. The young minister my friend called his mom and told her what was going on.she told him to come home that I was practicing witchcraft. As he told me what she said and told me not to touch him. I told him it was not me it was Gods doings. As he was talking to his mom on the phone the Lord said touch him and when I did he was slain in the spirit while he was still holding the phone and when he came to himself he ran out the door. And when he came back in he said for me not to touch him.I again told him it is not me it was GOD he said G OD told him to go in a closet for seven days and pray. Little by little people started to wake up and we just marveled at the work of God and gave thanks. Another time I was at home cleaning and some people from the church came by and we started to pray one of the men was cripple very badly his hand and foot was twisted.as I begin to pray for him as I was lead to do.my foot and hand begin to twist and the pain was horrible. After the prayer was over I told the man he said he lived with that kind of pain every day. One day my Lord spoke to me and told me that Fridays at church was Miracle day so I told my Pastor he allowed me to do as I was led to do on Friday so I started making me a dress the night before. As I was working the table that I had my sewing machine on began to shake. First I thought it was an earthquake. Then I saw some little imps little creatures running under my table. First I thought I seeing things then I begin to get scared. Then the spirits said wake up someone and have him or her to read from the bible. As you work I tried to wake up my oldest but she would not wake up. Then I woke up next to the youngest daughter she came into the living room. And laid on the couch and started to read. To me and kept falling to sleep I keep calling her name to wake up. And read because I was scared she tried I just called on the LORD. Finally I finished the dress and went to bed. Sometimes all of my kids would sleep in our bedroom no the floor and one morning Sherri next to the oldest said she seen Jesus standing over my bed and the number seven aver my head. I said thank God I didn't under stand what was going on but I thanked God anyway. God has done many wonderful things in my life even though I have been week and in the flesh. The next night at church we praised the LORD and God had his way thank God. My second to the oldest went on to Germany and God continued to bless us inspite of our self. She got married and her first born was a beautiful son. I continued going to church and taking my children with me sometimes my son would go also being tricked by the flesh and feeling bad about going to church and my son selling drugs and about me allowing it instead of praying and asking God to help me. And tell me what to do I have into trying to do it myself. What a nightmare I went to the Pastor. And told him how tired I was of being responsible for my husband. And all the responsibility I had with no help and about my son. I told him I felt like I should stop going to church because of what was going on with the drugs and all.I got back into drugs real heavy selling weed using the gift of knowledge that God gave me for evil. Thank God he loves all of his children.I began to toot coke again it helped to numb me. And I didn't feel much and didn't think much when I was high. The police came after my son and I hired a good lawyer and a bondsman to protect my son, and my people.I took my mom for her first limo ride out to the circle star theater,people started coming up to my car.I thought they thought I was with the show. Until they started yelling Mama Soul. And trying to get into the car. The devil will pump you up to fool you into thinking you have power. I thank God he is long suffering. I thank God he forgave me for putting my self and my son before him my faith was weak and I was without spiritual knowledge may this book open some eyes stand your ground for rightness. Believe God for all things, he can save your family, you can go to him for the smallest. For how to raise you child, getting a job was to live. Problems with your neighbor or your husband. Drug problems, strength to live right. Nothing is to hard, if you if you only believe God for it, you will have it. Call on God.ASK God IF YOU ARE DOING the right thing.. Ask him to lead you in all things. And wait for him to answer, be patient trust him with all your heart. And watch God work. Please don't do as I did and make a mess of your life. And then go to God, go to him first. And if your life is already a mess asks him to fix it. I am a witness that he will fix it for you. And when all have left you. He will never leave you, and will for give you for all your sins. No matter how terrible. He will not keep throwing it in your face, what you have done. He will give you another chance, again and again oh praise his name. Nothing is to small nothing.is to big or to complex to. High or to low trust him in all things have the faith the size of mustard seed. Try it Christ will not fail you. Even when we fail Christ will not fail he is all ways with you. Just call him and wait for him to answer. Be patient and watch and pray live holy some times we are made to believe that it is hard that is just Satan and he's lies don't do like me and fall for it then the turf wars begin to get worse and worse. While I was at a funeral at church the police raided my house. And someone called the church and told me.I rushed home even through people told me not to. I didn't want my son or family to suffer for my stupidity.I was told that guns were drawn on everyone in the house before I came. They even went next door to my mom's house. There were drugs there so they had arrest mom also. I told them everything in both houses was mine just mine and no one eases. They gave me a paper to sign and I did. Then I was hand cuffed and when they got ready to take me out side to the police car. There were over a hundred people and more coming. Trying to stop the police from taking me to jail. Why because I had done some good in my rain of crime. I would feed the needy families by taking around baskets of food at Christmas time. Get some of the young men out of jail.God will always take some thing bad and turn it into something good. I told them not to worry I would be all right and if they tried to stop them I would be the first one to die so they backed up. I told my mom how sorry I was for her going to jail. She said that was okay, she didn't mind.she was the first one out that's the way I wanted it. The charges were dropped against her. Because I said every thing they found was nine even though it was not mine. That was in her house. My stepfather was dying of cancer remember.he used it to help keep his food down after treatment. The police found guns and weed in my house I'm not going to lie to you I waved a jury trial and was sentenced to six months in jail.the first thing I said when I was locked up, is give me a cigarette.. Yes the food was so bad I would spend about a hundred dollars every two weeks at the store. Their was something like a rats limb found in the beans one day.I couldn't eat their food for a long while and when I did I looked through the food carefully.My husband was disabled. So the lawyer ask for leniency because of my husbands condition. He was a schizophrenic and had been since the age of eighteen. I ask his mother why she or his dad did not tell me since he didn't know? His mom said it was none of my business. They told him his medicine was for his stomach. The judge said no while I was in there my husband took an over dose of his medicine. He was in coma.the deputies called and told me that he was not expected to live.I asking for a modification of sentence. The judge said no I sent word to Charles that he had better wake up. And my daughter told him the way I said it and God blessed him to come out of it I also thought that money could buy what I wanted I ask the sheriff if I could buy and have prepared Christmas dinner for all the women in my dorm. He said no then I ask for all the women that was in jail.he said no I said how about the whole jail he said no. I think I was beginning to get the message. I was a good prisoner I worked when ever I was allowed doing what ever was ask of me mopping sweeping what ever. I seen women locked in padded rooms with no beds no toilet sometimes no clothes I t scared me. I asked why were they in there? The sheriff said they had problems something I didn't want to have. I would talk to my family they said every thing was okay. That was not true my son was selling coke now that how that money was being put on my books. My son told me that he had a problem with someone at a park and that he couldn't tell me over the phone but I read between the lines this is so hard to say he had killed someone. I got very upset and he said mom it was he or I. What could I do from were I was at when I got out my household was going crazy.my kids were during the best they could my husband was using coke with all the physic med. He was on none of the bills had been paid the house was going to be foreclosed. Charles my husband was receiving social security he had enough of an income to at least pay the house note. What did I do instead of going to Jesus I went to getting into selling coke when I say when I think of the goodness of Jesus and all he has done for me. My soul cries out hallelujah thank G OD FOR saving me.I tried to sell the house and HUD would not let me. I wanted to get out from under some of this pressure. I wanted to run but where could I run who could help me now. Most people were afraid to come near me unless they needed my help with a child or money. Some people had sons that they could not handle.so they would bring them to me. Because they seen the way my people would do as I said. And would brag about how good I treated them. Were selling drugs and I would help them on how to use the money for good that didn't make me a good person that was just good business sense. Flashback when I was going to church and living holy I had a vision the spirit of the Lord was high with me in church that evening and when I came home I was still in a special place in my spirit I laid down on the couch. And continued to pray and I open my eyes and I could see like a robe of someone standing next to the couch with out saying a word. I.was still in the spirit when I got home and was not able to change. All I wanted to do is lay down and think about the goodness of God and how good I felt so full of joy and peace I could feel the love of God all over me. As I lay there as I said earlier I could feel my spirit leaving my body.I looked back, as we were moving forward. The Holy Spirit that was leading me spoke no words to me. I was not afraid, we went down Gray hallway gliding not walking. Standing ahead of me coming into focus was cap wearing a pair of pajamas holding the bottom with his hand like they were loose he ask me what are you doing here? I said I was worried about him because I remember him saying he hated God. He said you would never guess whose down the hall.as he pointed down the hall with his right hand. Then I could feel myself floating back wards as he continued to say the same thing over and over.. As I slowly went back to my body.the next day when I told my son my dream. He was setting in his room with some of his associates. And he said mom if somebody killed me you would kill them for me wouldn't you? I couldn't say anything for a minute. He continued to ask me until I answered him.I said yes and in my heart I felt sad for saying yes.for me to promise to take a life was very sad. Yes I was using coke after I came home and dug into selling drugs again I was cooking up the coke of some of his workers and CO workers. The problems continued to get worse wand worse about the turf who could sell drugs were cars were being shot up boys were being shot and shot at. Charles had a dream he was shot seven times and didn't die. I also had a dream of me picking out my son's casket. The police had caught Charles but he didn't have any drugs on him. We went to court and he was given probation. And we were on our way home I was driving. I said I was worried about the girls if I got killed. He said don't worry about Stephanie she would make it. Here it is a beautiful day. Sun shinning not a cloud in the sky and we are talking about an untimely death. the way he said don't worry about Steph he had anger in his voice but I said nothing to him. I didn't ask him why he seemed so bitter to his sister. flashback my son had a very bad nose bleed. I couldn't stop it from bleeding.I rushed him to the hospital myself. Knew at that moment if any thing ever happen to my son I would loose it. What I felt at this moment was pain so bad I could hardly breath. I didn't take time to call an ambulance going so fast that I had to fight to hold on to the steering wheel.I was trying to be strong but I was scared to death.. They had to burn the inside of his noise to stop the bleeding I thank God that it stopped I was so tired I told the Lord as I cried out in pain to take my son I couldn't hold on much longer. On the way back from the hospital he bought me a teddy bear I felt so special. G

OD KNOWS I LOVED MY CHILDREN TO MUCH ALL OF THEM. During the turf wars I stud on the street at night with my son and his CO-workers by now we were all scared for our love ones. I was carrying a three fifty seven if I had shot and killed someone my God I would be in prison thank God he was still in charge I have never killed anyone. This went on for a while we got word that there was a hit on my sons life.I hired body guards for him he didn't want them I told them to go every where with him. Sometimes he wouldn't let them one day after we had been to court again. We stopped and had lunch after court. Charles said mom I'm tired I said do you want to go home and rest? He said not that kind of tired. I said do you want to quite the business? With hope in my heart he would say yes.he said no and we said no more about it. just tired and he drove and so he dropped me off at home. He had just bought a car from one of his colleagues and he wanted the title so he said he was going to his house to get it I said please don't go over on the turf looking for him wait for his bodyguard. As he left as always he blew his horn and waved at me little did I know that this would be the last time I would see him alive. I laid down on the sofa because I was very tired just wanted to lay down.I don't know how long I lay there before I heard someone calling me. Mama Soul Mama Soul I jumped up. And it was one of my sons friends saying Charlie had been shot I said was he dead? I could feel the fear and the rage building up in me.he said he didn't know but on this day my world stopped and I was lost and felt alone and confused he died this was May 29, 1984. In the mid afternoon he drove me over to the street. To an unpaved road we call the dirt road next to the road was a couple of homes. Charlie lay face down and dead on the side of the first house. I was trebling like a ten point earthquake inside and out. and like someone was stabbing me at the same time over and over with a dull blade a jagged blade. the police were there an ambulance was there. I could see my sons body covered up laying face down in the dirt.I have been told many stories about how and who killed my son. But the funeral home told me he had been shot by one bullet just a hair under the heart.. He was killed instantly I have no idea that pulled the trigger. The police showed me what they felt was proof who killed him. I don't feel convertible with nothing I have heard. One thing for sure he or they can't escapes God. God knows and we must all come into account for all. The most painful story I. was told by a young boy and that was he talk to Charles. And Charles asks him for a cold towel and not to leave him. Another said that Charles had made it to safety. And that he came back into the line of fire to help someone. Who I don't know. He was very loyal to his friends and I say that loosely.and when I search for the answer, I get a different answer each time.I can tell you standing there looking at my son laying face down in the dirt. Still knowing that he will never move again. Never answer my call.the pain is more severe than having a baby in hard labor.I just screamed again and again all I could do was scream. I couldn't breath I couldn't move I couldn't hear. No one could touch me my mother was there my husband Charles my son's stepfather was there with me. I didn't care I was numb. Finally we left for the hospital I don't know how to this day who drove me or if I drove its still to painful and its 14 yrs. ago Later if you think I had a problem then I really went crazy after his death cocaine was my middle name. I smoked from sun up to sun down and all in between smoked up at least a new car or two we don't mean economy cars. And I'm not being funny or by no means bragging. Just trying to let you know how deep it was.if it was not for Jesus I would have had a massive heart attack from if nothing else but the drugs. I made the arrangements for the funeral and one of his Judas friends bought his suit for him to be buried in. the reason why I called him Judas is because he took my son over to the shooter house. And told the shooter that the one I shake hands with is the one you are to kill. I was told by a source that was and is believable. There were threats of coming to the funeral home and disrupting the service so we were prepared we had security every where some of his friends that wanted to come I didn't let come for a host of reasons one is I couldn't tell friend from foe. His grave is not marked to this day I will mark his grave this year if the Lord says the same. After my son died I sold more coke than ever before no one was going to stop my son from selling where ever he wanted I don't mean the police I mean the gangs that were taking over different areas that were coming from different places, even other towns.I was told that there was a contract on my life.I didn't care, one of the boys came by and told me he seen some one on the garage roof behind me. He said the man on the roof was wearing a fatigue out fit. So he would not be so easily spotted. At my kitchen sliding glass door.I tighten up security, I had seven soldiers living in my home around the clock. And one setting in the kitchen with a shotgun around the clock. He was never off just relieved for rest if you think it took a lot of money it did. But I was not trying to save money I spent it as fast as I made it. There was a time when I wanted revenge for the death of my son so bad that I could taste I wanted blood to run.I called a meeting of all the boys that were apart of the family. And told them that I wanted the person that killed my son to die and all his people. The ones that we thought it was sent word back that they didn't do it. Now I feel so bad that I could have that kind of rage inside of me to even think of doing harm to anyone no matter what had happen.I thank full that God is merciful. And under stands our inter most feelings.he knew that deep in my heart that is not what I wanted I was just in pain. I started to thinking I wanted no one to go through the pain that I was in.it was not worth it little by little my family left me I was smoking more and more before I new it I was alone. Still in business but not like before I was getting tired. And wanted to quit but was told I had to many people depending on me for me to quit. Then my mother died of cancer I had no idea until almost the end thank God she didn't suffer a long time on the ride moms last ride the police stopped the limo and searched it. Why I don't know why I was just numb. Probably because I was in the car. After mom died I was alone no one seemed to really care it seemed but little did I know that God was always there for me all I had to do was call on him. A lady came to my house I didn't know her she was so nice just out of the blue offered her help even told me where I could get deal on coke I should have known it was a set up by now I was selling just for my habit I still was able to help people who needed food or something flask back one of my neighbors we will call her miss M. came to me because she was about to loose her home.she said that if I gave her some coke, I could take over the house notes on her home.she came with proof in her hand I was so scared. I told her there was no way, I would be a part of any thing like that. I didn't know what to do I tell her No. And told her she had better get it together because had young children. And one very special child who needed her more because he had special needs. She had a very bad coke or shall I say drug habit. She would do all kinds of things so my son and others told me. Such as having sex with the drug men so that she could get drugs. They would ask for all kinds of favors let your mind run wild. I did care enough to stay on her case to do better.she would go and get her drugs were she thought I wouldn't know but I did find out.one day she came running down to my house for help.She said her son was sleep, and she could not wake up.I ran to her house, beating her home. Her 13 yr. Old son was on the sofa I touched him he was dead. I was told he died in his sleep having a seizure. After that she got worse and lost her home and moved away. And later I was told she died from a drug over dose. After she moved one day I was laying on the bed and I heard some shots and I told my daughter to call 911 that some one was shot on the corner how did I know. God only knows there was a young man lying on the sidewalk he had been shot. And there was very little blood I held him in my arms and he died. flash back when I was seeking the Lord and living for him, as I should have. He told me to go to the same street were this happen and pray. I would go up and down the block and pray. Not out loud like to draw attention to my self but silently. And I did not think or care that people might think I was crazy. Later as things happen I realize that it could have been a lot worse if I were not obedient to God. And prayed for my brothers and sisters, who lived and were in the areas in the time of trouble. I'm sure somebody has, and is praying for me. And to God be the glory, I truly thank him for my saved life thank God for not giving up on me. When I left him after all he has done for me. I thank him for welcoming me back again and forgiving me again and again. More people could have died or been hurt even the day when one man was shot there was about six people standing by. Also after Miss M. moved they found a dead body raped in a rug in the garage. Just less than ten feet from the shooting were many home. I rushed around there and guns were drawn. I stepped in between them and begged them not to fight.I kept talking until they cooled down. I believe God was dealing with me and giving the courage to try and get off the madness of drugs and would let me see what drugs was doing to me. I was in so much of my own misery of my own doing that I refused to hear what God was telling me. Then I heard that greed was coming more between those that had been hustling side by side. I called them together and ask them if they wanted to see their families go through what they see me going through behind the death of my son. Please don't misunderstand stand it was not me it was God working through me remember God rains on the just and the UN just we are all his children and I thank God he was there was no blood shed that day. Some times I was able to break through and not use drugs by the Grace of God. God would speak to me but I just didn't break loose back to the lady she called someone and we went to meet with him and do a drug deal.I could feel that it was not right. But I went anyway. It was about 9pm when we left my house and went over on the other side of town. When he came he said we had to go in his car. When we got in his car I felt like I was in trouble he told us to wait in the car he had to make a stop while he was gone I tried to get out and couldn't. She said she was trying also then I begin to feel sleepy. Some men came by in a pickup truck a d I heard one say Mama Soul I said that was strange. A few minutes later he came back to the car and said we were going to his father house. And we did he invited us in to the house. The man had two of the biggest dogs that I have ever seen. He offered us coke I said no thanks he said are you sure I said yes. And to myself I said if I'm going to die I'm going to be sober.I should have been asking for forgiveness of my sins. I was to blinded I should have been thinking of my soul. His Grace has given that thank God I'm still here. and. After we left there it was about am then he said we had to make one more stop to pick up the drugs? We went to a small apartment and he woke up some man and told us he would be right back and they went outside to talk all three of them.I sat in the chair knowing that some thing was going to happen to me. This place was dirty and the furniture was broken down. A door open and only one person came back in.it was the one they woke up he just sat there. He looked like a cold-hearted guy. He also looked like he would not have a problem to kill me. He acted like a hard smoker skinny dirty under his nails. His hair hadn't been combed mated to his head. Skin looked dried out lips looked burned. Clothes had not been washed lately. We didn't say too much to each other.it got to be a few hours later he started nodding off to sleep. I was very quit hoping he would finally fall off to sleep but he didn't so I said I was going outside to get some air. He said that his landlord would not like it. I said I would be very quit as I moved close to the door. I made my way out the door and ran until seen a cab hailed down the cab and went home. I have not seen or heard from her as expected. Trying to break away I dressed and went to a shopping center wearing a lot of my diamonds and gold. I don't know how long he had been following me but I'm sure I was a good target with all that on and being alone.he spoke and we had a casual conversation about the weather etc..he was about 5 feet 5 inches and small frame.I didn't feel threaten at all he ask me out. I said no we kept on talking it was a very nice day and I was enjoying it. Little did I know the danger hovering over me? I ended up giving him my phone number and he was to give me a call some times. Which he did we go out that night visiting his friends? I took my car so I would fill more in control. What a joke I went to take him home and pulled up in his driveway he lived in San Francisco. We sat for a minute then some one open the back door of my car. And said don't look around I have a gun at both your heads. Some one else got in on the other side. They said start up the car and go where we say. By now I felt like I must really have a death wish. And I had no doubt I was going to die. We drove around as they talked about were they were going to take us. So we parked by a park and across from the park was a hospital. As we sat in the park they taped our hands and feet and were going to take the car. I told them that the tags were expired. And if they took the car the police would get them. He-said take off all your jewelry. I took it off some I stuffed in the seat behind me. As I started to take off my gold around my neck.he snatched it off my neck so hard it burned. Then they decided to leave us bound and tied and through the car keys out the car and for us to wait a couple of hours before we move. As they were leaving a car pulled up next to us a couple of seniors were in it they looked and pulled off. After the men left my date said we better not move I told him what he could do. And I ran to the hospital and they sent for the police. After I gave my statement I went home and told my boys that were on the corner. They went looking for them and found one. And he talked I got all my jewelry back except a small amount I was happy he was arrested for bank robbery charges he was wanted for before he robbed I dropped the charges the police was very upset and wanted to know how much I was paid. I said nothing I lied. I got a full white mink coat after that I got worse and worse. Me using drugs I couldn't shake it. And when I tried all the memories came back. I pond all my diamonds and gold and smoked it up every thing I could get my hands on. I stopped trying and gave up.one day the police came with a warrant for my son. I said he is dead It was like being stabbed with a sharp ice pick with a hook on the end.so when you pull it out it will take some of you with it. Let me tell you that the more you give the devil the more he will take. Give him a ride he will want to drive if you let him drive he will put you out and take your car. And try and kill you at the same time. But remember that God the only true giver of life. The only one that can allow you to die. God has the last word and I thank him.if it were up to man we would all be dead from greed and jealousy selfishness hatred. I sold every thing I had that was valuable and smoked it up. I had nothing left I had just heard that it was said that I had my son selling drugs for me. That almost drove me crazy then I heard that I sold my next to the youngest to the dope man. God is my witness I did no such thing how can people be so cruel to say such to this day it hurts. I walked away from the shell of a house. And went to Hayward to my daughters fighting to get off drugs. Before I left Oakland I was standing on the corner talking to one of the fellas. And a man came up and ask me were he could buy drugs. I set it up and was busted.got out on bail and went to Hayward. I thank God I had somewhere I could go inspite of my problem. I never stole from any one in the family I thank God for that I always had money enough. Or someone gave it to me. Missed my court date on purpose I told my bondsman. He elected to get me other dates as I hid from the police. One morning as I went to the store, for my daughter to get some milk.I met a man name, can you believe named Charles.a third I must have been drawn to the name. we were waiting for the store to open it was a nice day the sun was shining warm on me. there was not a cloud in the sky. I was clean not under the influence of drugs. He said his dad was a preacher and his mother was the first lady of the church.. I was so happy I felt that I was on the right track I told him what was going on in my life I did a lot of talking it felt good I should have known that something was wrong when he never mention God. I don't care who they say they are, if they try and hold a conversation with you and don't mention God. When you are talking to someone about serious problems. And you tell them how lost you feel and how bad the pain is. And Gods name is not mention that is a problem especially when they claim to love the Lord. Bells should go off, especially if you are telling them about all your trials tribulations. we talked for hours and he told me he was on the run for drugs. And left out something very serious. He took me to where he was hiding out. Which was his sister's garage, I ask him why didn't he stay in her apartment? He said she didn't't want him to, he said he was waiting for a delivery from the dope man. After a while he said he was going to get us some food from his mom. When he left out of the garage I heard the police calling him. I could hear him running waited for a while until I didn't hear anyone. Then I left I went down the street to see if I could see him.I seen a lady walking looking around like she was looking for someone. I ask her if she was looking for someone? And I told her mine name and she said she was Charles the thirds mother.She invited me to her home and I told her that I was on the run. From the police for drug charges. She said that her son Charles was too. Mother G. As we will call her was very nice to me and allowed me to wait for him at her house he took so long I went home. When he came home to her house they came over to my daughter's apartment were I was staying. It was safer at my daughter's house than hers for Charles. I told them that I wanted to leave the area Mother G said why don't you go to Lakeport near Clear lake its nice and quit up there I said I wanted to get off drugs and get my life back in order and start living for the Lord again. His mother was pleased with my suggestion she said yes baby that would be good. I said I didn't want to go alone Charles said he would like to go with me. I had a small income, that Charles the second had set up for me, so that I would have some kind of income to help me. Charles was saying, all the things I wanted to here. How he was going to get off drugs and get his life together, and that we where going to be together. Just the two of us and we were going to make it work. How we were going to enjoy living in Lakeport. That we both could get a job, and be comfortable, His mom said she would help with food and whatever she and her family could. His family drove us up to Lakeport. And I took some coke with me I had told Charles that I was going to bring some with me. And that after we finish it I was not going to do drugs. That I was going to quit for good. So when we got there after his family left we did smoke the coke. After we finish I ask him to take the pipe out side and break it. That I was finish don't think he believed me. The next day we had a good time. We went to the store we had a room with a small kitchen and two plates and a pot and a skillet and our place was very clean and bright. Which I loved, we walked a lot we had no car so we walked or used a cab, since I was our support for everything our money was very limited. Charles the third had no money and had no wish to get a job. After we got tired of watching television, I rented videos because, I didn't want him to leave me alone after a few weeks of this, he went to take some videos back, in a cab but after he didn't come after a few hours, which only takes a half hour, to take them back, and pick up more, I thought he had gotten caught, by the police. I cried all night.I called his family, who didn't seem to be surprised, not, that I wanted him, In my sight all the time. But I knew nothing about this place, he sure did he say that his family came up here a lot to fish. After a few days, he came back like he had just left. I can not even remember the lie he told me. I was so -apply to see him I didn't say anything, I kept my word, to my self and God, I didn't go back to drugs, of any kind. After that he would disappear every few weeks. I excepted it for a while, then I found out how he was leaving town. We moved to Nice, because it was cheaper, we moved into a nice cottage, right across from the lake, It was a beautiful view, from my living room. It really was peaceful His family came down his mom and dad to go fishing, he had disappeared, so we had a good time any way. He started staying away longer and longer, I wanted to know how he was getting around with no money. Then one day he was setting in the living room, while I cooked his dinner, someone knocked at the door, he rushed to get the door and went outside, with no shoes on, and he didn't come back. I looked out side and didn't see him, but I know I heard a woman's voice. By now I know that he is playing me. When he comes back about a week or so later, he tells me that he is using her for us I said no, but I knew that he was lying to me. This went on and on I stopped arguing with him about her.I didn't want him to use any one, would I refuse to let any thing, send me back to drugs. No matter how much, it hurt. And believe me, it hurt, to know he was using me.I would not, let the devil, destroy how far God, has blessed me to come. I kept my promise to my self and God, and never used drugs again, no matter how hard things got and believe me, they got hard, and I let him go and come with out saying any thing.all though he knew that I was angry and disappointed with him. I was not ready to give up yet. I hoped he would see how much I cared for him. And would return the feelings that is a mistake. I have made the same mistake over, and over again a person has to want what ever God is offering. Just like trying to save some one that we love or care for because we know that Jesus is the only way, and his gift is eternal life. Only God can save, or give the gift of love, love is a gift, from God.He also gives us free will to except his way or our. This went on and on finally I said I was leaving him. I told him I no longer wanted to live together, that I was giving my life back to God and that we had to marry if we continued to live together. Wishing this is what he needed to get a reality check and start living according to Gods word.He said yes lets get married and that he loved me and that it was just the other women's money. And he was going to stop seeing her. So we married and surprise nothing changed but you knew it was not I was the only one that refused to see him for what he was. He got arrested for shoplifting why because he was running out of cigarettes. Not for food we always had food by the Grace of God. Knowing that he was wanted to go in a store and steal a carton of cigarettes, to me is a cry for help unless you want to go back to jail. God blessed him he went to jail but they let him go and didn't check state wide for warrants I know that he couldn't have forgotten we both were wanted. So what happen to him thinking about what may happen to me if he went to jail. He continued to go and come whenever he wanted, from me to her back and forth I would set and cry for hours. I would think about taking my life, it was so messed up I felt so lost and hopeless. But again I made the same mistakes. I kept hoping and praying that he would change for the better never happen. We moved to Tracy I was so happy to move close to people, I really was very happy, we lived in a city again. Charles still didn't look for work he always had an excuse for not working I finally realize he must have felt he was to cute or that he was being slick, but he didn't fall under either one. For some reason I just had strong feelings for him. I think I just didn't want to be alone but what a price to pay just to say you have some one that you are with. When he was home he would always say I was cheating on him and that I would bring men home when he was not home. That I was going to bed with them In our home.God is my witness I never had any one or even thought of having any one any where. I was always faithful to him. If only I had learned to put my trust In God not man because God will never let you down man will.My walk with God I was seeking more of him. And he was drawing me closer to him, you know sometimes we can get ourselves into so much trouble. That we just can't jump out, being entangled with the yolk of bondage. By that I mean the trouble we get our selves into. I really liked our apartment it was up stairs and had a very nice view of the mountains. A large one bedroom And In the bedroom I had a special place where I would go and pray. God was giving me strength to continue on.he lead me to a little church, This church had only about six or eight member.The church looked like it could hold about thirty people. Charles would go to church with me sometimes, sometimes not; he was still seeing the other women going and coming whenever he liked. I was getting a little stronger by the Grace of God, and I thank him for never giving up on me, that's the kind of God we serve he is great and long-suffering. The pastor and his wife were very nice to us both.we would go out to there ranch for dinner often and he had another church in another town not to far away. We would go with them to service at both churches and I was allowed the privilege of teaching bible class sometimes and given the keys to open the church. I didn't tell the pastor that we were on the run from the police but I think he knew it some how And Charles would lie to them so much sometimes I seen the pastors face. Charles is very gifted he can play several instruments. He would often go to church with me. Sometimes, he would play the drums, sometimes, the piano, sometimes the guitar, he is very blessed, While we lived In Tracy I was still waiting on a settlement from my loan company I had been awarded, God has supplied my need all my life. He loves all his children and knows their heart. While waiting I had received a letter giving me a date that I would get the money so I had a plan.I didn't wait to get the money before I started spending just being stupid and impatient. God says be impatient for nothing. But I was so I wrote checks for things I wanted for the Holidays thinking that I would have money to cover them. Also I needed my California ID to get a job, While at D.M.V. the clerk told me that I had a failure to appear which I of course new about It was my drug case. In other words I was wanted. Which I already new that I was wanted I got a lump in my throat because I knew that I was going to be arrested soon because I had to give her my address. I was sure by now that the bondsman was looking for me also I was getting tired of living like this on the run I wanted to see my family my kids. Charles the third was not any different he was doing the same thing had finally been able to get a few nice things for our apartment. And some nice clothes not expensive or fancy, just something to wear to church, and look right, you know what I mean? I hope. One day we were just laying around the apartment, We heard a knock at the door I got a chill I knew that it was not his family who would sometime come and bring us groceries. I said who is it he said police and I knew it was for me I said may I get dressed after I let the officer In he said okay, just don't run I said I would not. Charles told me to run but I was tired of running and hiding I wanted this over. While at the police station I had to call the pastor to come and get the keys for the church and to tell him and the first lady what was going on. They received it well and were kind and gentile to me. And ask if I was going to be all right. I said I would be fine I was scared. But I didn't tell any one, I know that they could tell I was shaking, I had to pay for what I did. I was not going to trust Charles, with the mail box key, to get my checks.I explain to the pastor and his wife, if they would do so. And told them what I was expecting, they said that they would, do what ever they could to help. So off to jail I went I didn't know what was going to happen to me I didn't know if I was going to the pen or what. First they said three years, I said no way, for one twenty dollar, rock of cocaine, I was set up any way, but that was okay. I needed to get this over with, because I was a drug dealer. Even if this time it was not my drugs. I had been getting away, with selling at other times. Let me tell you what happen I was not selling drugs this day and it had been a few days I was wearing down I wanted out of this mess. I didn't't want to go on.I had stop paying, the house notes long a go.I didn't have the will, to keep fighting. Charles the second had went his way.I ask him to; he had a drug habit. Doing things I would not do. Such as heroin and cocaine mixed, and he had someone he was seeing. Don't get me wrong cocaine alone is a very dangerous and additive drug, and will kill you quick. But to mix it with anything is suicide. Now remember he was on very strong, mental health medicine also. I just couldn't handle things any more. He had to take responsibility for his own life. One day some of the people that like to hang around, for whatever reason free drugs or what ever. Some I believe like being around me, I hope. This night in particular it was about eight, in the evening.we were waiting for drugs to come available, just to use not to sell this night. The light was dim in the room everything looked dingy and dirty looking.It was clean, but dirty from all the smoking of cigarettes and drugs. Am I making my self-clear? We started talking about Jesus, I felt bad, talking about him, and how I had been living. I thank God he never leaves me, or forsakes me. He knew what I was going to do, before I was in my mother's womb, and he still loves me. My God I thank you for your love in the name of Jesus Lord I give thanks Amen. This drug house. As I looked up at the curtain it seemed to be shaped in the face of

Jesus. I could see the face as clear as if someone painted it on the drapes. I will never forget, the look as long as I live, God is my witness. No, I was not high, It was very plain, and I ask anyone if they could see it? They said no.In my mind, I said Lord why is your face to wrinkled? And full of pain. He spoke back to my mind, and said this is the pain, you are causing me. I will never for get that, a little while later I don't know how many days later I was alone at home and walked down to the corner I said hi to all the fellas out that night. And went to the corner store and got some chips to eat I didn't eat often. When I came out of the store some men were trying to buy drugs, I told one of the fellas let me sell it to him so I could make the money and have some free drugs too. To keep my supply for my self he said okay, I sold to an under cover officer and went to jail.I was bonded out in a few hours I just called my bondsman to come and get me, he was on retainer. So that was how this case happen.I fought In court for months and had money kept on my books so I could have yarn to make things. But while in jail waiting on God to work it out I started going into the room where the boiler was it was a room where You could hang socks to dry after you washed them out. There was barely enough room, for one or two people. So I ask a lady, if she wanted to go in to the boiler room, and pray with me. And very night, about six or seven, we would go in and pray. We didn't tell any one, we would just do it. Then others started asking, what were we doing.I told them, some ask if you are a Christian, and are saved, why are you here? I explain that I was there that I was not always saved but I am now. Then one by one more would try to get in this little room. We finally had to go out into the dorm were we slept. Before I knew it, one by one, we ended up with one hundred and twenty three women, praying and receiving prayer. God moved in wondrous ways.

After that women that were looking, at being there for the holidays, were set free, some were afraid to leave, when they called out there name, for release. I can remember one night; God woke me up, and said to call the women to pray. This was after lights out, but I did what God said, and one of the deputies came and called out the lady, we were praying for. When she came back, she said they told her, that her father was very ill, we prayed for him and her family members. I held Bible class, one day a week. And lived the life before them. Stayed In the word and stayed prayerful. One day we were knitting and crocheting, and doing our hobbies when one of the ladies said mom would you ask God to fix the heat, he will answer your prayers. When ladies came in, I would do what ever I could, if needed try and get blankets. Because the heater would go out, and it would get very cold, cold like snow country. The women would leave our dorm, and go out to the other dorms, after they were sentence. They would see me in the window, or at mealtime, and tell me that they were keeping the prayer line going. Some of the ladies were being release to the street and said they would continue to live the life before God. I received it by faith and prayed they would continue to follow Jesus. I was talking to Charles, on the phone he was upset, because I was not calling him more. And that I didn't let him get my check every month. But I paid the rent, while I was in jail.I didn't want to stop, and think what he was doing while I was there. I just kept running for and living the life and sharing Gods word with who ever wanted to hear and was very happy to do so. The pastor and his wife came to see me, and always ask, was I all right.I said yes, the pastor ask are you sure I thank God for them and knowing that they cared was a blessing to me. By the time I went to court by the Grace of God I was given six months and credit for time served. After that I was brought to what is called North County, a jail in downtown Oakland. No more prayer circles or group prayer, this jail everyone was locked down, like in the pen, I am told. I thank God I have never been to the pen. When I was released the pastor and his wife picked me up. The pastor had been holding a check, which came while I was there. I ask him to just hold it, until I got out.I went to cash it, it was for about twenty five hundred dollars, thank God for that. After I cashed it I paid my tithes first.God has always put me first.For once I wanted to give him his due first. When I walked into my apartment most of everything was gone. Including clothes, shoes, bedding, dishes, VCR and television etc. he had sold it or traded it for drugs just cried He was gone with his women he was not at home to even greet me. I don't even remember what he had to say if anything about what he had taken and sold. After that we moved to Tracy, I bought a car. And came back and forth to my probation officer in Oakland, until I was off. Now I had a clean record, I thought had for gotten the checks I wrote.now I had to fight this, maybe go back to jail. This time it would be the pen, for sure. I thank God for his mercy and his love for his children. I went to the attorney, and told him the truth, about waiting for a large check, and thinking it was going to come on time. I had letters from the settlement attorney, and told him, how I got caught up in the holidays, and I had every intention to pay for everything had plan to have the money in the bank before the checks started to get there. I didn't even get the clothes and things, until two days before the check was suppose to come was hoping, and thinking, that I would make a deposit before the checks reached the bank. But I was so tired of fighting I said whatever happens. I took a letter over to the lawyer to show him what I said was true. And I had just said to my self what ever happens I will just deal with it because I did it to my self. Charles the third was right there he was just waiting to see what was going to happen, so he could go to his other women, I guess. I was starting to feel like a life less thing not even a person; I was not feeling sorry for my self I was just tired of fighting for a life. I just didn't know where to start to get my life back together again if I ever had one I work hard when I can find a job. Then one morning, I got a call from the lawyer, saying that they were going to drop the charges. I thank God but I still was in a deep depreciation I couldn't seem to get out of it and I couldn't find my way out of this pit I was in.I needed to pray and to have some one pray for me. Where could I find prayer, I couldn't, I was so bound, I couldn't seem to reach out for help. There didn't seem to be any one, to pray with me. No one, came up to me, and said let's pray. Little did I know that all I had to do is ask Jesus, to help me? We were at my daughters, in Hayward. For a minute, then we went back to Fairfield. I worked, very hard, in Fairfield, as a temp at Clorox, Jelly belly, and for an inventory company. Where ever I could find work. I just couldn't seem to find a permanent job. Charles was not looking for work. As usual same old excuse, that he was wanted. He had become a very heavy weight, on me. But I ask for him, to be in my life, so I just had to take the weight. AND WAIT, ON God, to deliver me, out of another mess. I had gotten my self, into again, when will I learn? I have searched the world over looking for love in all the wrong places. Little did I know that love was with me, all along.I really thank God, that he is long-suffering? I thank him for his love, for his children, me included. We finally moved from Fairfield, back to Hayward. I was very happy; I wanted to be near what family I had. That allowed me, to be a part of their lives. My daughter Terri was, and is always there, to help me move with her children, my grand's. I lived with Terri, for a while and Charles went to jail. He was charged with rape. I was in shock I didn't believe it, I stood by his side through it all. I excepted his calls, I wrote to him; I tried to encourage him. I moved, from my daughters to my brothers. I couldn't find work, at all. I went to the welfare for help; I had no income at all. While on welfare, I went to the gain program, with the hope of finding a job. But instead they put me to work, for the welfare in the office. Filing papers, answering phones, sometimes working with client's papers. To pay back the three hundred dollars I received every month. I loved the fact that I was working but I was not getting anywhere I was told that the county was not hiring so don't expect to get hired by them. The way I heard, some of the social workers talk about their clients. Really hurt me, and busted my bubble, about people that did this kind of work, were all people that wanted to help. That they were most all, any way was, and they're for the money. And don't really care about the clients. From what I heard them say, the clients were not, even people in there eyes. I heard one say that the women should be treated like animals because that's how they breed, that they should be castrated. I felt like crying, I was so hurt, by the remarks. I had to listen to this every day and could not respond.. There was one social worker that had work to be done from nineteen eighty something this was in early nineties up grades for more food stamps or more aid because the situation had changed I did listen and learn. I continued to go to school also to become a computer technician learning to do software and repair them set up networking I received all kinds of awards for perfect attendance and for achievements and so on, I was really trying hard. I wanted a life; I wanted to be able to work. I had started going back to church and really did all I knew how. I cried out to Jesus, and ask for an apartment, of my own. I really needed my own, I never felt needed at anyone's home, or wanted. Unless I had money to give them for staying there. You can tell, when you are wanted and needed.I wanted to get a good job, I thought I would when I finished school, computer Techs are in demand. With all their awards, that I would have no problem, finding a job. I was not looking to start at the top. I just wanted a chance. First of all I prayed for an apartment of my own I spent a lot of time crying I really am a very sensitive person well God answered my prayers again, How many miracles can I have? I moved in an apartment with only an income of three hundred dollars a month, I started my own business of helping people find houses and apartments which by the Grace of God I was able to pay the bills. Charles the third was still in jail. Also I started receiving a check every two weeks, I moved from the one bedroom to two-bedroom townhouse in another complex. I was very happy to be in my own place I tried to get a room mate, that didn't work out.So I lived there alone and went to church. I kept looking for a job, especially in the computer field, still no luck. I turned the second bedroom into an office for me I was pleased with it.A lady came to me for help in finding an apartment, she needed it in a hurry. She was coming out of a fifteen-year marriage and had to move and was left with a lot of problems. She explain to me she was of Moslem belief, I ask God what could I do, to help her, through him, God blessed, I was able to help her find an apartment, and at the same time we became friends. She has two daughters and she is a good mother. We have a lot in common about child raising. We both are very old fashion, about school, dating, clothes, etc. plus other things. I did my very best to live the life of a holy, and God fearing women, before her. And shared a lot with her, about my husband and what I had been through with him, and that I had to wait, on

God, to release me, from the marriage.if it was to be a marriage or not to be no. Matter what he has done. He got out of prison, and the same time he got out, she the other women picked him up from prison. I didn't even know that he was out of prison. He started all over again; I didn't see him until he was out about a week or more. He would come in, and out, of my life, as he seen fit. I kept praying, and going to church, and seeking more of God. And had peace in the mist of my storm. When he would come home, his family would call him for her. She would call my home for him, to meet her. She had a man; she was married to or living with, for many years. Some say he is a dangerous man.She would come to my home, with some of Charles family, and set outside, until he would go out. Sometime the police would come to the door for them. She was said to have family on the force. I had a hard time, understanding, how a family would do this. But I understand this woman had money. She worked at an abortion clinic, she had no children of her own I still held my peace not out of fear from them but God says hold your peace and I will fight your battles, and I did. One day I was in prayer at morning prayer when the Lord spoke to me and said he was taking Charles, I was frightened for Charles because I didn't know what was going to happen to him I told his mother but I don't think she believed me. Then all of a sudden, Charles came over, and said he was coming home. For the first time, in our marriage, he brought all kinds of things. Such as a television, his clothes, birds etc. of his, Said he loved me, and was sorry, for the way he had treated, me all these years. I forgave him, He left, he said to go pick up some money, or something, he never came back again. When I heard from him again, he was in jail. On his way back to prison, for rape, and the woman was said to have aids. He told me about it he said he didn't rape her she was mad because he ran out of drugs divorced him after that, I started to get my life together again and started trying to understand what I have been doing to myself. I had so much pain and hurt from looking for love and approval from anyone that would give it even if it meant allowing my self to be used by them. So that I could pretend that some one really cares for me, even though I know that they didn't. All of my life I have wanted to be loved by someone, and be loved in return just for being me. I don't think that there is a person that knows my favorite flower or my favorite color what are some of my special things to do. Or what makes me laugh or what makes me happy what my dreams is IM not feeling sorry for my self just stating a few facts. Well then I decided to get into the apartment management business. Finally I landed a job as an apartment mgr. Of a small complex I was so happy to be doing something I wanted and proud of my self that by the Grace of God I got the job. I didn't make much money but when I did the extra work like painting, cleaning apartments after the people left Don't get me wrong it was very hard work carrying five gallons of paint up and down stairs patching walls cleaning parking lots etc. One apartment had a thousand dollars worth of work to be done. Including taking wallpaper off the walls, which happen to be a jungle scene, trash, and etc. Worked seven days a week, I went on a shopping spree after I finish that one. I needed to, and a lady I knew from shopping at the store where she was the ass. Manager, said what you need, is a man, I said the only man I want is one that loved me enough, to show love, like a picture we seen of a man kissing, his ladies leg so tenderly. Learn not to speak it into coming true, you may get what you ask for. I had to go into an apartment with one of the maintenance men to repair a stove, and this man answered the door with no shirt on.I had never seen him before and he was not on the lease. I ask for the lady I rented to he said she had to go to work and he was a friend of hers that he was just coming off a three day job as a long shore man. I didn't know what that was but I said to my self that it is nice that some one had such a hard working man. He was very friendly and I could feel him staring at me it gave me goose bumps, he has a very soothing voice. After that we would talk every day and I really enjoyed it. It felt good, to have someone to talk to, and who would listen, and really seem to listen to what ever I was saying. He is really an easy person to talk to. I have never had any one that I could talk to and who seem to listen. Finally he made his move, and said I was going to be his lady. I said no thanks; I had been hurt enough. And I was not looking for anyone. That it had been a few years, since I had any one.In my life and that I believe in living a celibate life. And that means no pre marital sex. He was very patient with me, he had a plan, He has mingled gray hair, a nice round firm tummy, not belly just a nice curve built solid tummy.I thought he was in his mid forties, or early fifties. He was loosing his hair, he was half bald, which didn't make me any difference was still fighting him, I refuse to see him, on any grounds, other than as a friend. One day he came over and said, what can I do to help you.I said nothing, I am doing fine, I don't need any help, but thanks for asking. He was standing so close that I could feel his breath on my neck. It made me shake a little. And I didn't understand this feeling because I was not going to let myself get involved with him or any one. He got closer and kissed me. I didn't know how to respond. I didn't want to get involved. I didn't want to except what I was feeling. I was so silly that I ran into my apartment. Into the bedroom of all places I didn't think he would follow me in there. He followed me I said don't touch me. And ran into the living room, really fighting my own feelings for him. I was ready to cry I didn't want to care for him or no one. He left and I cried like a baby. After that I didn't see him for a few days. I hated to admit it but I missed him. Not talking to him, He always said don't worry he has my back. No matter what, I even told him about my life, in the super fast lane. As soon as I got a hold on what I was feeling for him, here he comes again. Here he comes again.I said we could only be friends, he said okay. I felt relax, He asks me if I would take him to a record store. He wanted to pick up a few tapes. I said sure, I believe he said that his mom was using his car. That he needed it right now.I never gave it a second thought, that he was not being truthful with me. We went to the record shop and I picked a few tapes, and so did he. We went right back to the apartments after that.He started calling me every day. And soon we were going to the movies. And going to the bowling alleys while he bowl. And to baseball games of little league were he was the empire. I really started to enjoy my self, more and more with him. We would go and set at McDonalds just to be together and we couldn't go to my apartment it was just across from his girlfriends. After weeks of this we said that we would go to a motel just to set and watch movies and have dinner together. Yes I believed that was going to be all-right, We shared paying for our evenings. The night we went to the motel I was shaking. I said I was not, going to let anything happen between us, no matter what.I was going to stay in control, We had ordered dinner, and turned on the television. And I reminded him that I was saved, and didn't believe, in sex before marriage. By this time I was so in love with his lies, that I couldn't stay in the control, that I hoped I could. I really was a very lonely and needy woman. I was not prayed up I didn't have on the full armor of God as I should have. He said I am not going to force you to do anything, you don't want to. It was my own fault that we made love. I should never have gone there with him. I okay and began to relax and he said could I hold you I said just hold me he said okay that was another big mistake. The passion was very over riding my every thought, and before I new it we were making love, I felt sad and happy at the same time I felt like I had let God down and I cried. Had let God down again this time I knew that I was in love with this man. I ask God for Mercy and I thank God for his Mercy. WE started spending a lot of time together, he was still seeing her but IM not good as the other women or sharing. And I told him we could not live together. He had to make a choice and if it was I we had to get married. I was not going to add to my sins by living together. Warning started going off in my head but I was in love with whom I wanted him to be not who he was, I heard what I wanted to hear. I felt like I could Pray him into heaven kicking and screaming he was not going on his own, Then one day I let him use my car to go to work he said. I didn't see him for three days. I was scared that something had happen to him I called his mom she said she had not seen him. I was worried sick, I had no idea that he was on creak cocaine. I called the police not to report it missing just to see what I could do. The officer was very nice, we talked a while, and I gave him all of the information about my car and about my man. He said if he seen my car he would talk to When E, came home I could smell the cocaine on him. I was so wrapped up in him. All I could say is IM glad you are back. And why didn't you call? I told him I would not leave him, because of his habit, that I would try and help him if he wanted help. He said he was stopping no more drugs, he knew how to make up. All of a sudden it was my money we were using for everything clothes and groceries for his two children he had by someone else. Yes two very young children. Under five both of them, He said that his clothes were over his mother's house that he didn't keep anything over his ladies apartment. He kept going back and forth, from me to her; does this sound like something I just came out of? By the time he ask me to marry him, I found out that he was younger than I, and that he had no car, and no money. And that he didn't work, many days on the waterfront. Because he had to wait for a promotion, to up grade, to get more jobs, Also I found out that he was the sweetheart of the lady that had become my friend while I helped her get an apartment. I found out because she and I talked a lot, and E and I talked a lot, even though he stretched the truth a lot. We will call her Miss. Kim she was a Moslem.She had found, someone special in her life also.I ask her, after she gave me a picture of herself and her new love. And E seen it, and said that, he and Kim were lovers. But when I ask her, she said it was not a serious relationship at all. That they were school kids about sixteen years old.I said for her to please tell me if it was serious she said no. I E started calling other women from my house. I could not believe that I had gotten into such a mess that was going to become a horrible mess. I could go on and on but, when we went to Tahoe to get married, all the way there he was so strange.He didn't seem like a man, that was about to marry some one he loved. He was very with drawn and didn't seem or act in the least bit happy. When we got there, and parked in front of the chapel, we were in Tahoe. He said he could not go through with it. I was very hurt and confused. I said okay take me back to Oakland. We went to a parking lot, and he left, and when he came back he said he was ready. I said I was not, just take me back to Oakland. He said he was ready, and for us to go ahead with our plans. Hearing what I wanted to hear and not all the warnings going off and the sludge hammer hints in my head. He said he was not leaving until we got married. Again I hear, what I wanted to hear, he had no money, no ring. I paid for the whole thing I was really hurt. But I felt like that's what I deserved.On the way home, we stopped, and I bought some pictures, for our apartment. A week later, he was talking on the phone to someone, and told him or her while I was cooking dinner. That he was not happy, I guess they said he should leave. That's what he did, he got up and packed the clothes I had bought for him. And even took the pictures off the wall, and moved back, to his old girlfriend across the driveway. Now this is a small complex and everyone knew what happen. I could set in my living room, and hear them laughing. It felt like I was being stabbed, with a jagged knife over and over. He came back, and I got fired from my job as manager. And he left; again I had to find a new job. I ask him if he would help me? And go on interviews with me.I finally landed a job. First I had to fix up, and rent out the entire apartment in a nine-unit building. It was in terrible shape, located in East Oakland. It had one and two bedroom units. Some of the units had to be painted, wholes patched up, trash removed, carpet shampooed. Cars that had been left on the property removed. Then I was promised a very nice seventy-unit complex. When and if I did a good job on the small one, I did all the work myself except for towing the cars away. I had to find a towing company to do it for me and I did. The company I worked for was so surprise, and told me that they had never seen it so clean and nice. E said he could not live in Oakland. He didn't like that part of town. He would just drop by to see me not staying. Finally I finished the job. And went on to the bigger complex.. E thought he was going to be on salary. Like I was but they just added him as my husband. And said that any work he did that was extra; he would be paid separate. He was very angry. Behind my back he told them that we were not together, and tried to get the job from me. It didn't happen, one of my bosses told me what he was trying to do. He didn't have the experience and they wouldn't allow him to try. I was very embarrassed when they told me what he said I worked very hard and also tried to help a lot of people get a second chance at a nice apartment. I did so well at cleaning, painting, repairing, and getting the apartments rented. That they ask me to help with other complexes, that were having trouble. E was going back and forth, between his other women and home. With me his wife as he pleased and he had what it took to be a very good bowler. And I tried to help him, with money to play, and try to encourage him to join the P. B. A. I spent a lot of money and we traveled a lot. So he could try and win at different tournaments. But it seemed that he would do just fine until he was close to winning and he would drop off like he was afraid of winning. I did all I could to encourage him and keep him pumped up he would get a call or call someone and that was that. The only time he won was once he won about a thousand dollars them he paid off his mom money he owned her? Then the kids, me last, I didn't say anything. When we were not on the road, he was with the other women. Some I met on the road, he had different ones in each place, were he bowled. But he was single than, before we married. He had never been married before. Many wanted to marry him. He is a handsome looking man. I was not looking at him that, way until we were already in a relationship. Believe it or not it was his voice that was so soothing, to me and what he said, just what I wanted to hear. One day we were talking and he confessed to me that he loved the young lady that he had two children by I ask why did he marry me he said because I said we couldn't live together unless we were married and he didn't want to loose me. And that he was with the other woman for sexual pleasure only. Many hours I sat at the bowling alley, with him sometimes taking my work. There were always reports to do; l also took bookkeeping, with me. Sometimes I would set at the hall in my car for hours, to see if I could drive him to a job site. So that he could or would work would set in my car at the longshoreman's hall for three or four hours waiting. Very seldom would I let him use the car because he would disappear for days and I had to go to the bank and other complexes for my job. He started talking about a truck, and I wanted a new car. Yes I took about three thousand dollars I was saving and I alone bought a car and a truck. He took the truck and went over to his girlfriends and stayed for a few days as always when I would call over there he would say hi like he was just visiting a friend and nothing was wrong. Sometimes I would go over there and tell him to give me the keys. One day coming out of the main office door I slipped and fell on my back. Down some concrete steps, that was the beginning of another down fall. I had to hire people to do my job, because my back was in bad shape. But that's what happens when we say, Lord, IM turning this part of my life over to you, But IM still handling this part myself. What you get is a mess, God will just wait for us to finish making a bigger mess, and listen for our cry for help, and because he loves us, he comes running to our rescue to fix the trouble, we have gotten into if we let him. Remember we have free will. We either let go and let God have his way, or do it our way that is our choice that God has given us. I thank God that I am learning to allow his will to be done in my life. No matter what it is I will seek God for what to do, about anything. From what to eat to what to wear what to say and to hold my peace and let him fight my battles. I learned the very hard way that nothing is to small or to big or to complicate for God. If we just remember that he is our creator. There is nothing that he does not already know about us. He knows every thought word and deed. When I stop to think that he chose me while I was yet in my mother's womb, It makes me feel very humble because he knew what I was going to do before I did it. And yet he loves me in spite of my self." Lord I thank you". I know that I am yet learning and will continue to make mistakes. But all I have to do is ask for forgiveness and guidance, wisdom and knowledge, believe Romans 10:9,10 and It shall be given unto you. God will supply all yes all my needs. He has proven it over and over to me. E didn't come to my rescue and help. My doctor wanted me to quit my job I said no that I had worked to hard to get where I was and I didn't want to give it up. I kept going to therapy and trying to work as best as I could finally the doctor sent a letter to my boss saying that I had to be on light duty. More trouble begins, the boss started complaining about my job. Sayings I didn't keep it clean enough. Than my paycheck was wrong. Than they acted like my deposit slip for the bank was missing. None of their plans worked. I was good at my job and God blessed me with a good business head and a clear one for business, thank God for that. I always had backup files, and was well known at the bank. I was always able to find the deposit slips for them. That would seem to make them angry. I really always had the energy to fight hard in the business world when ever I was given a chance to shine I loved to be complimented on a job well done I would work even harder. I had to even hire someone to clean my apartment because I worked so had I didn't have the energy to do it myself. Guess what some of my suits and dresses came up missing and I didn't know it until after. One of my housekeepers was stealing and the least one that I suspected.My back was getting worse and worse. And my boss knew that, one day out of the blue they fired me I was so hurt because I worked very hard for them first they said I was not doing my job than they said I stole money from them. I knew that if they had thought that they would have called the police so fast. I never stole one dime from them and they knew it but they fired me because they could tell that I was going to have to give up my job soon because my back was getting worse I could hardly walk. By the time they fired me I was managing or help in managing four complexes three was at least seventy-five units. I also help to sale the nine-unit complex not even thanks. Without a notice I was fired and told to move out in three days but the devil is a lie it took me a few months to move. They kept taking me to court to evict me. God had mercy and softens the heart of the Judge each time I went until I found a place. Well need I say E. was no where to be found for any help He took the truck and left. But God is a good God he gives you what you need when you need it Thanks to my daughter Terri, and her kids, which are my grand's. I was able to move and I paid some other people to help also. I was in such a poor condition my back was so much pain to take a step went from my neck down my spine. I was not able to walk a block with out such pain that I felt like crying. Sometimes my knees would fail and I would fall. After I got moved In I sat and cried I ask God for strength to go on even though I wanted to die. I didn't feel like I could start over. Where do I start? What can I do? Lord your will be done, give me strength. I cried and prayed, and ask God for help to make it. I kept going to church and prayer, until I was not able to go up and down the steps. So I shut in and read my bible, and prayed, and fasted. I refuse to take any pain medicine because I needed to hear from heaven and I didn't want to be light headed. Don't get me wrong I was In so much pain It hurt just to get up to go to the bathroom. Some times I couldn't get up to fix me something to eat. And I had no one to bring me something to eat. People had all kinds of advice as to what I should do but God said hold my peace and he would fight my battles. Well I did pray and then I filed for a divorce. And the friend we call Miss Kim served him for me at his girlfriend's apartment he was shocked he said. I gave him the truck and told him he had to make the rest of the payments I gave him all his clothes. After that I promised God the father I was not going to do it again that if he didn't send someone in my life that I was not going to. God sent me word not to get entangled again with the yoke of bondage, by a man that had ask me out I said no that I didn't date. E came over and he said at first that he was going to stop the divorce, then said just kidding, at night I cried out in pain. The back pain was horrible but I didn't want to take drugs. I was seeking more of God and wanted to keep my head clear I just prayed and cried out to my Heavenly father and he gave me strength to make it night after night. One day a friend gave me about seventy pieces of fried chicken. I didn't want to see the chicken go to waste. So I called someone and they said they couldn't use it. And why didn't I take it to one of the parks and give it to the people. And I did, that started me on a journey. I started feeding the people at the parks, or wherever I seen or got a call for help. Seven days a week I went to a bakery and was blessed with all kinds of bread and pastries. I got so much that I was able to go to areas that needed a helping hand and would pass out the food. Most of the time I went alone, and it was very hard for me to carry the bags. But God is a good God and gave me strength, at night some times I would hurt so bad from carrying food up and down the stairs but I just kept going because I knew that people needed the food that I was blessed with. This brought me so much joy to help people. I didn't mind hurting and doing with out to help others.It made me feel like some one needed me, and depended on me. Come rain or shine I was there. All my life I have always love to give.It gave me such peace, I know that it is a gift from God, and I give him thanks and all the glory and honor. I have learned from the gift of wisdom from God s daily anointing of wisdom through prayer, fasting and studying Gods word that my brain can hold that I must pray for daily. Is that what I need cant be bought with money. Only through the will of God can I have what I need and I must strive daily for my flesh to die to what It wants in order for Gods will to be alive In me. Yes I have wishes but God is and must be first in my life. If it is his will that I have these wishes then so be It, If not I ask for strength, to receive what God says, and praise him for it and give thanks. I wanted others to see Christ in me, and that I really love him because he first loved me, and to know that he gave his only son so that we may live. I had one son and he was murdered, but God loves us so that he gave his son for you and I. All praise and honor to him. God open up doors for me I gave the car back mainly because I was not sure what E. might try since I was foolish enough to put his name on it also, that he may try to take it. I just didn't wish to have it any more. I felt like I could use that money for my friends at the park. My income was barely enough to pay rent I didn't have a hundred dollars left. God open up a door financially, and I got another car kept feeding my friends at the park E. said he would help yes he was still coming by. I explain to my friends at the park that I didn't have much more than they did but God was making a way for me to feed them I real loved it. It was hard seven days a week I went to this bakery and picked up bread and rolls and sweets and got a routine going. I would feed them two or three times a week at least one hot meal a week. Ounce in a while I could get someone to help me carry the food down stairs not to often. Then three or four times a week I would take bread and sweets to different areas and give away bread and what ever I had. Every dime I could get my hands on I would buy food for my friends I knew that God was going to open another door for me if that is what he wanted me to do. But in the mean time I did all I could do. I prayed a lot, and stayed in the Bible, I seem to be getting closer to my heavenly father. Doing all I knew how to do to stay repentful. One day my friend Miss Kim called as she did often, but this day she ask me if I would come over to her house and talk to her and her boyfriend. I explain to her as I had done so many times before that I don't believe In people living together.She said she knew but they needed help, that they loved one another. She needed me to help,I ask God what could I say or do? I knew that God would have to word my mouth, and give me wisdom. I told her to ask her boyfriend if he would like for me to come over and we have a counseling session.She ask him he said yes, he knew the lord and knew it had to be a change In their relationship. I went over nervous I had no idea what God was going to do through me. She gave her heart to God and they repented of their sins and excepted Jesus as their Lord and Savior,Praise God.She had been a Muslim for about fifteen years.God is a good, yes he is. they got married twice one was so that God would bless the union of them living together and the second one was so that family and friends could be a part of it.They are still living as husband and wife and going to church and reading the word and praying to the Father through our Lord and savior Jesus Christ. E. and I slept together as husband and wife twice after I filed for a divorce. I ask God to help me and he did after that we did not sleep together again. We can get into a mess by our self, but only God can get us out, leading and carrying us through it all. Only God has the patience and Love we need to make it. And to know that he never leaves us, nor for sakes us, gives me the strength to go on. As I sat at the kitchen table and read the Bible with Bible tapes to help me better with the Hebrew words. Being able to say the words made me understand better. I went to church but I was in so much pain it was hard to set long. But I pressed my way on and I continued to feed my friends at the park there this went on for about eight months, non stop. Sometimes I would have Bible study at my home and a few people would come. the spirit of God would come in and we would have a time in the Lord. Prophecies went forth through some for others me included. I was no longer able to carry the food up and down the stairs. I could not stand and cook for my friends. I told the Lord if it was his will for me to stop to make it plain to me. The Lord started dealing with me about the prophecies that had went forth on my life. Some at this time I will share. Some I do not feel lead to share right now, but I promise to share with you later. One promise was a new home, a husband that loved the Lord, anoint my ministry with more power from on high. financial blessings and there is more which I promise to tell you later. One night in a vision God spoke to my mind and said that all that had been told to me would come to pass. How Many Miracles can I Have? I know that I am loved by God just like you. God is no respect of person, we are all the same in his eyes. The more you get to know him the more you will love him. His love for us is beyond our understanding. Just think about it God allowed and gave his son to be born suffer and to die so that we live. how great thou art oh Lord. God works in mysterious ways, I was waiting for the Lord to lead me to what he wanted me to do next. One day one of my brothers brought a man by that he had been playing golf with. He and I got along very well from the start we spent many hours praying and sharing our testimony what God has done for us and what God was going to do. Wait! I am getting ahead of the story. I started not paying attention to the way I was eating and I went on the cabbage diet, but I ate a lot of watermelon and other fruit with has a lot of sugar. Then I stayed so thirsty and drank a lot of water, it would run right through then I started having problems with my sight it became very blurry. Then I got a yeast infection.I went to the emergency room several times.finally I ask that my sugar be checked after a friend of mine said it sounded like diabetes. When they checked it, it was four hundred and something close to five I believe. She meaning the nurse that took the test made a surprising sound and went to tell the doctor. When the Doctor came in he said that I was going to have to stay. I said I didn't want to stay, he said he knows but I must stay that I had diabetes. that they needed to get it under control. Yes I was scared, But I knew that God was in charge of my life and what ever he said all I needed was for him to give me strength to receive his will. I knew and know that I was and am saved and repented of my sins. I also knew that I had and have more work to do so I could not die even if I wanted to. How did I know God had told me. I knew that my body was and is in a very delicate condition, so I said your will my father. I he next morning I woke up to God speaking to my mind saying again that he was going to do a new thing. I trust and believe in God with all of my being no matter what people say and do. God has always been there for me and loved me in spite of my self. I was a very bad patient I refuse to except what the doctors said. If God didn't say it I held on to the word of God. Again I must tell you that God had told me something's he was doing and going to do in my life and I received all of what he said no matter what any one said including the doctors. I was sent home after three days and my sugar was the same level it was when I went in. The doctor in charge said and I quote your good times are over she said as she got up very fast and left the room. she seem to be very up set, my God bless her. The hospital had made arrangements for a visiting nurse to come, and check me every day. When she came after I told her that I was not on medicine, she became very upset. she called the hospital and made arrangements for my meds. I was finally put on a strict diet and four shots of insuln a day. I gave myself the shots as the nurse told me. I started going to a doctor in Oakland. I told him what I knew what one very important thing was going on with my body besides the diabetes. of course he rejected all I said that was okey, God will have the final word so be it because God cant lie. The nurse came every day once a day for months. I just prayed and gave thanks to God for all things and I told God I knew that I was healed. And when I was ready to line up with his will I would not have to take the insulin. I cried every day because it was me that had not done as I was told. How to eat and live by the will of God. This went on from June to February, the nurses would come and daily I got stronger and more stable by the grace of God. I would tell them when they came that Gods will be done, and that I was healed. they would try and tell me things such as when your kidneys fail or your liver or you cut you self what was going to happen. My Peter spirit would rise up and God would calm me down. And then I would speak the wisdom God gave me. That I lived by faith and that I was already healed That I was waiting for God to say when I could stop taking my insulin. I continued to be obedient and take my shots and eat the way and time I was to most of the time. Then one morning I was blessed to minister to and be minister to by someone. we started early one morning and God had given us our portion for the day. and we feasted on the goodness of God for hours. Then I realized that it was about two and a half hours late for me to take my insulin shot. I told God In my mind as I continued to give my friend what God had told to me to say. I said Lord you are just going to have to keep me healthy until I finish your work. then I will take my insulin, God spoke to my mind and said I didn't have to take it any more. Tears started coming down my face, I said how great thou art Lord you have such Love for a person like me. I told the man I was ministering to what God has said, Im not sure what he said I know we were both happy and praising God. Feb. 4,98 was my last injection. I never went back to the doctor, he never call to see why. I told all who would listen not to many shouted for joy, not all believed IM sure.

But I thank God and will serve him all of my days and will tell the Good News that Jesus Christ is Lord and that he loves us in spite of our self. God can and will take something bad and turn it into something good, if only we will allow his will to be the head of our life. Some people still ask am I still heal with joy I tell them as a bull, by the Grace of God. There is so much going on In my life God gets closer and closer as I live the life and praise him daily. I give thanks daily for my portion of him and I ask for forgiveness, because IM not perfect but IM striving for it. Jesus said be yea Holy as I am holy. I die daily to what the flesh craves for to become stronger in and closer to God I read and study my bible so I can learn more of him. I need him I cant and have no desire to live with out him. I have so much more to share with you, but it must be later my friends. Please be encourage and continue to believe, thrust, hope and know that All is possible with God, If you hold up God will show up, and he is always on time. And will never give us more than we can handle. I am learning this more and more and more. God every day opens a door for me to have my needs met, he fights my battles for me and you if we hold our tongue.

My God bless you and give you what you need. I will be writing you again soon my friend.

## About the Author

This is the first of a two book autobiography.

It is as you will be able to tell is a very strong, but very honest book about my life, by the Grace of God I lived through it.

I believe all that read it will be Blessed in more than one way.

I hope you take the time to read it, I know it will be a best seller.

www.ingramcontent.com/pod-product-compliance
Ingram Content Group UK Ltd.
Pitfield, Milton Keynes, MK11 3LW, UK
UKHW040559210726
13854UKWH00008B/1552

9 780759 674684